10/09

DATE DUE

DEMCO, INC. 38-2931

1st EDITION

Perspectives on Diseases and Disorders

Allergies

Clay Farris Naff
Book Editor

Detroit • New York • San Francisco • New Haven, Conn • Waterville, Maine • London

Christine Nasso, *Publisher*
Elizabeth Des Chenes, *Managing Editor*

© 2009 Greenhaven Press, a part of Gale, Cengage Learning

Gale and Greenhaven Press are registered trademarks used herein under license.

For more information, contact:
Greenhaven Press
27500 Drake Rd.
Farmington Hills, MI 48331-3535
Or you can visit our Internet site at gale.cengage.com

For product information and technology assistance, contact us at

Gale Customer Support, 1-800-877-4253
For permission to use material from this text or product, submit all requests online at www.cengage.com/permissions

Further permissions questions can be emailed to permissionrequest@cengage.com

Articles in Greenhaven Press anthologies are often edited for length to meet page requirements. In addition, original titles of these works are changed to clearly present the main thesis and to explicitly indicate the author's opinion. Every effort is made to ensure that Greenhaven Press accurately reflects the original intent of the authors. Every effort has been made to trace the owners of copyrighted material.

Cover image Custom Medical Stock Photo, Inc. Reproduced by permission.

LIBRARY OF CONGRESS CATALOGING-IN-PUBLICATION DATA

Allergies / Clay Farris Naff, book editor.
    p. cm. — (Perspectives on diseases and disorders)
 Includes bibliographical references and index.
 ISBN 978-0-7377-4377-7 (hardcover)
 1. Allergy—Juvenile literature. I. Naff, Clay Farris.
 RC585.A3437 2009
 616.97—dc22

                                         2008042979

Printed in the United States of America
1 2 3 4 5 6 7 13 12 11 10 09

CONTENTS

CHAPTER 2   Controversies About Allergies

CHAPTER 3 Personal Experiences with Allergies

FOREWORD

"Medicine, to produce health, has to examine disease."
—Plutarch

Independent research on a health issue is often the first step to complement discussions with a physician. But locating accurate, well-organized, understandable medical information can be a challenge. A simple Internet search on terms such as "cancer" or "diabetes," for example, returns an intimidating number of results. Sifting through the results can be daunting, particularly when some of the information is inconsistent or even contradictory. The Greenhaven Press series Perspectives on Diseases and Disorders offers a solution to the often overwhelming nature of researching diseases and disorders.

From the clinical to the personal, titles in the Perspectives on Diseases and Disorders series provide student and other researchers with authoritative, accessible information in unique anthologies that include basic information about the disease or disorder, controversial aspects of diagnosis and treatment, and first-person accounts of those impacted by the disease. The result is a well-rounded combination of primary and secondary sources that, together, provide the reader with a better understanding of the disease or disorder.

Each volume in Perspectives on Diseases and Disorders explores a particular disease or disorder in detail. Material for each volume is carefully selected from a wide range of sources, including encyclopedias, journals, newspapers, nonfiction books, speeches, government documents, pamphlets, organization newsletters, and position papers. Articles in the first chapter provide an authoritative, up-to-date overview that covers symptoms, causes and effects, treatments, cures, and medical advances. The second chapter presents a substantial number of opposing viewpoints on controversial treatments and other current debates relating to the volume topic. The third chapter offers a variety of personal perspectives on the disease or disorder. Patients, doctors, caregivers, and loved ones represent just some of the voices found in this narrative chapter.

Each Perspectives on Diseases and Disorders volume also includes:

- An annotated table of contents that provides a brief summary of each article in the volume.
- An introduction specific to the volume topic.
- Full-color charts and graphs to illustrate key points, concepts, and theories.
- Full-color photos that show aspects of the disease or disorder and enhance textual material.
- "Fast Facts" that highlight pertinent additional statistics and surprising points.
- A glossary providing users with definitions of important terms.
- A chronology of important dates relating to the disease or disorder.
- An annotated list of organizations to contact for students and other readers seeking additional information.
- A bibliography of additional books and periodicals for further research.
- A detailed subject index that allows readers to quickly find the information they need.

Whether a student researching a disorder, a patient recently diagnosed with a disease, or an individual who simply wants to learn more about a particular disease or disorder, a reader who turns to Perspectives on Diseases and Disorders will find a wealth of information in each volume that offers not only basic information, but also vigorous debate from multiple perspectives.

INTRODUCTION

Ten-year-old Peter sits alone in the lunchroom. The Massachusetts schoolboy is not unpopular, he just cannot risk sharing a table with someone who is eating peanuts or peanut butter. Even a whiff of the stuff could send Peter to the hospital. His classroom has been made a nut-free zone. The whole school may soon follow. Peter is just one of nearly half a million kids in the United States who are allergic to peanuts.

Most kids love peanut butter, but PB & J sandwiches are rapidly disappearing from school lunchrooms in an

Between 1997 and 2002 the rate of adverse peanut reactions in children doubled, prompting researchers to study allergies associated with the peanut.
(© Enigma/Alamy)

attempt to protect the apparently growing number of children who have life-threatening reactions to peanuts and many other commonplace foods and items.

"We've heard about parents complaining, 'What do you mean I can't send my child with peanut butter and jelly?'" said Mary Mcdonough, whose daughter has a severe allergy. "If they were with me on the rides to the emergency room or sat with me for the eight hours that they were watching her, maybe they'd change their mind."[1]

Reports of peanut allergies—or, more precisely, adverse peanut reactions—in young children doubled between 1997 and 2002. Many people, including some pediatricians, believe that this rise reflects an epidemic of allergies of all kinds.

"Allergies are definitely more prevalent today,"[2] physician Marc Rothenberg, chief of the Allergy and Clinical Immunology section at Children's Hospital Medical Center of Cincinnati, tells Parenthood.com. In fact, Rothenberg says, the past five decades have seen tremendous growth in the incidence of all immune-based diseases, including allergies.

A Tangled Web

Sorting out the facts from the fears is no easy task. In the first place, although the symptoms of a severe allergy attack and a severe food reaction are virtually the same, the underlying pathologies are quite different. A genuine allergy occurs only if the body's immune system—specifically, a part of it called immunoglobulin E, or IgE for short—reacts to some normally harmless substance, such as pollen, instead of remaining on alert for a virus or other invader.

IgE is not involved in what most people call food allergies, so these are technically sensitivities or adverse reactions. Still, the outcome is much the same: Symptoms range from mild irritations—itchy lips or other body parts, skin rash, or wheeziness—to life-imperiling reactions such as a throat that swells shut or a drop in blood pressure so steep that blackout and even heart failure may follow.

Why different immune pathologies should seem to be on the rise simultaneously compounds the mystery—and gives rise to skepticism among some scientists. Maybe, the skeptics say, the apparent rise is actually a case of increased reporting or even overreporting.

For whatever reason, the attention paid to food "allergies" has rocketed in recent years. By one estimate, more than 90 percent of all research papers on peanut reactions have been published just since 1995. Parenting magazines abound with cautionary stories and stern advice for anxious parents about danger lurking in the fridge and food cabinet.

Disputed Numbers

The evidence for an actual rise in the number of allergy sufferers is murky. Many researchers believe the numbers published in the media are exaggerations. In America these range from 30 million to 50 million (9 to 16 percent of the U.S. population). A European study found that 15 percent of parents report that their children suffer from food allergies.

However, rigorous studies do not support such figures. They suggest that no more than 2 percent of adults and 8 percent of children have genuine allergies. The higher figures may come from sloppy diagnosis, media hype, or mere hysteria, researchers say. One problem is that while genuine allergies can be diagnosed accurately with a skin test, the clinical diagnosis of food sensitivities is much more subjective. The anxiety of parents and children, and the natural desire of a doctor not to wrongly dismiss their concerns, can lead to false positives.

In any event, the risk of death has been exaggerated, experts say. Official records put the number of food-allergy fatalities at a few dozen per decade. Those figures

are disputed by some advocates for allergy sufferers, but figures from other countries seem to bear out a low number. In the United Kingdom only eight children died from food allergies between 1990 and 2000, for example, and similar figures are reported from Sweden and Canada. By contrast, food poisoning kills about five thousand people a year in the United States alone.

In Search of a Cause

Fatalities may not be commonplace, but there is evidence that allergies are, especially among children. A Michigan study of public schools found a relatively low rate of food allergy among schoolchildren there—less than 2 percent—but they were widely distributed. More than one-third of the schools surveyed had at least one child with a food allergy. Studies such as this make it clear that whatever the precise numbers may be, the problem of allergies is something that all communities will have to respond to—at least until medical science can develop an effective treatment.

If allergies are indeed on the rise, we are far from knowing why. After all, the immune system has evolved for millions of years. Why should it suddenly start to malfunction? Scientists have some hypotheses—educated guesses—but so far none has been backed by solid evidence. One of the leading ideas, termed the "hygiene hypothesis," is that our modern environment has become too clean. No rise in allergies has been observed in places where kids grow up in environments where modern hygiene is unknown.

The immune system has evolved to battle dangerous invaders such as parasites, viruses, and bacteria. But modern sewage systems, handwashing practices, and the widespread use of antibacterial soaps and sprays have sterilized the environment that many children grow up in. Their immune systems fail to encounter a wide range of germs early in life, and without these intended adversaries, some say, the immune system starts battling the wrong targets, such as peanuts, milk, or pollen, instead.

Another hypothesis holds antibiotics to blame. "By upsetting the body's normal balance of gut microbes, antibiotics may prevent our immune system from distinguishing between harmless chemicals and real attacks,"[3] the *New Scientist* magazine reports. An unintended side effect of many antibiotics is to kill helpful bacteria that live in the intestines. That is why diarrhea is a common side effect of antibiotics. However, the possibility that long-term use of antibiotics may touch off an allergy is now emerging. Citing research by Gary Huffnagle of the University of Michigan, the magazine claims that experimental evidence in mice shows that upsetting the gut flora can provoke an allergic response.

According to some researchers, Caesarean section, or C-section, births, in which a baby is surgically removed from the mother's uterus, are to blame. C-section deliveries, which have risen 40 percent in the last decade, may put babies at higher risk for allergies, perhaps because they are never exposed to healthful bacteria in their mothers' birth canals.

Whatever the reason for the apparent rise, allergies certainly cause widespread suffering and social dislocation. While pills and shots can bring temporary relief, what people really want is a cure. Whether that hope can be fulfilled, only time will tell.

Notes

1. Quoted in Sydney Schwartz, "Schools Balance Students' Appetite for Nuts, Allergy Worries," *Quincy (MA) Patriot Ledger*, March 15, 2008. www.patriotledger.com/news/x1302483386.
2. Quoted in Parenthood.com, "Why Are Allergies on the Rise?" special report, 2008. www.parenthood.com/article-topics/article-topics .php?Article_ID=4228.
3. James Randerson, "Antibiotics Linked to Huge Rise in Allergies," *New Scientist*, May 27, 2004. www.newscientist.com/article.ns? id=dn5047.

CHAPTER 1

Understanding Allergies

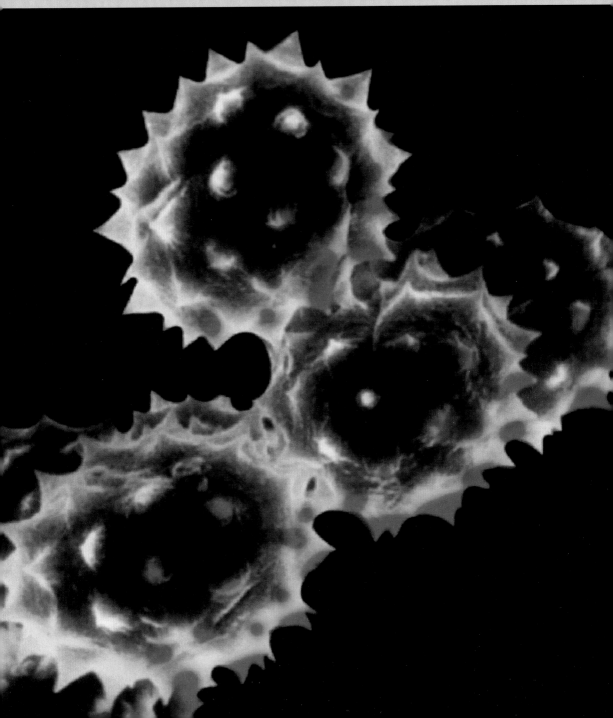

Allergies: An Overview

Richard Robinson, Jill Granger, and Teresa G. Odle

Allergies are among the most common and most mysterious of maladies. In the following selection from the *Gale Encyclopedia of Medicine*, the authors explain that allergies are a malfunction of the body's immune system, which normally protects us against invading pathogens. When the immune system mistakes a harmless substance for a germ, an allergy results. It can be either an instantaneous or a creeping reaction that takes as much as several days to develop. The symptoms of an allergy run the gamut from mildly irritating—runny nose and itchy eyes, for example—all the way up to a life-threatening swelling of the throat or drop in blood pressure. Although diagnosis and treatment are possible, the best prevention according to the selection is to steer clear of whatever substance causes the allergic reaction in the first place. Richard Robinson, Jill Granger, and Teresa G. Odle are writers and editors of the *Gale Encyclopedia of Medicine*.

Photo on previous page. A microscopic view of pollen, the main nonfood contributor to allergies. (© SuperStock, Inc.)

SOURCE: Richard Robinson, Jill Granger, and Teresa G. Odle, *The Gale Encyclopedia of Medicine.* Detroit: Gale, 2006. Reproduced by permission of Gale, a part of Cengage Learning.

Allergies are abnormal reactions of the immune system that occur in response to otherwise harmless substances.

Allergies are among the most common of medical disorders. It is estimated that 60 million Americans, or more than one in every five people, suffer from some form of allergy, with similar proportions throughout much of the rest of the world. Allergy is the single largest reason for school absence and is a major source of lost productivity in the workplace.

An allergy is a type of immune reaction. Normally, the immune system responds to foreign microorganisms or particles by producing specific proteins called antibodies.

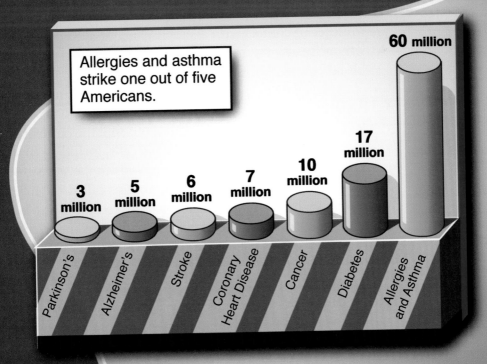

Allergies Are Among the Most Common Ailments

Allergies and asthma strike one out of five Americans.

3 million — Parkinson's
5 million — Alzheimer's
6 million — Stroke
7 million — Coronary Heart Disease
10 million — Cancer
17 million — Diabetes
60 million — Allergies and Asthma

Taken from: Asthma and Allergy Foundation of America. www.aafast1.org.

These antibodies are capable of binding to identifying molecules, or antigens, on the foreign particle. This reaction between antibody and antigen sets off a series of chemical reactions designed to protect the body from infection. Sometimes, this same series of reactions is triggered by harmless, everyday substances such as pollen, dust, and animal danders. When this occurs, an allergy develops against the offending substance (an allergen).

Mast cells, one of the major players in allergic reactions, capture and display a particular type of antibody, called immunoglobulin type E (IgE), that binds to allergens. Inside mast cells are small chemical-filled packets called granules. Granules contain a variety of potent chemicals, including histamine.

Immunologists separate allergic reactions into two main types: immediate hypersensitivity reactions, which are predominantly mast cell–mediated and occur within minutes of contact with allergens; and delayed hypersensitivity reactions, mediated by T cells (a type of white blood cell) and occurring hours to days after exposure.

Inhaled or ingested allergens usually cause immediate hypersensitivity reactions. Allergens bind to IgE antibodies on the surface of mast cells, which spill the contents of their granules out onto neighboring cells, including blood vessels and nerve cells. Histamine binds to the surfaces of these other cells through special proteins called histamine receptors. Interaction of histamine with receptors on blood vessels causes increased leakiness, leading to fluid collection, swelling and increased redness. Histamine also stimulates pain receptors, making tissue more sensitive and irritable. Symptoms last from one to several hours following contact.

In the upper airways and eyes, immediate hypersensitivity reactions cause the runny nose and itchy, bloodshot eyes typical of allergic rhinitis. In the gastrointestinal tract, these reactions lead to swelling and irritation of the intestinal lining, which causes the cramping and diarrhea typical of food allergy. Allergens that enter the circulation may cause hives, angioedema, anaphylaxis, or atopic dermatitis.

Allergens on the skin usually cause delayed hypersensitivity reaction. Roving T cells contact the allergen, setting in motion a more prolonged immune response. This type of allergic response may develop over several days following contact with the allergen, and symptoms may persist for a week or more.

Types of Allergens

Allergens enter the body through four main routes: the airways, the skin, the gastrointestinal tract, and the circulatory system.

Airborne allergens cause the sneezing, runny nose, and itchy, bloodshot eyes of hay fever (allergic rhinitis). Airborne allergens can also affect the lining of the lungs, causing asthma, or conjunctivitis (pink eye). Exposure to cockroach allergens has been associated with the development of asthma. Airborne allergens from household pets are another common source of environmental exposure.

Allergens in food can cause itching and swelling of the lips and throat, cramps, and diarrhea. When absorbed into the bloodstream, they may cause hives (urticaria) or more severe reactions involving recurrent, non-inflammatory swelling of the skin, mucous membranes, organs, and brain (angioedema). Some food allergens may cause anaphylaxis, a potentially life-threatening condition marked by tissue swelling, airway constriction, and drop in blood pressure. Allergies to foods such as cow's milk, eggs, nuts, fish, and legumes (peanuts and soybeans) are common. Allergies to fruits and vegetables may also occur.

In contact with the skin, allergens can cause reddening, itching, and blistering, called contact dermatitis. Skin

Airborne allergens from household pets are a common source of allergies. (© Bubbles Photolibrary/Alamy)

reactions can also occur from allergens introduced through the airways or gastrointestinal tract. This type of reaction is known as atopic dermatitis. Dermatitis may arise from an allergic response (such as from poison ivy), or exposure to an irritant causing nonimmune damage to skin cells (such as soap, cold, and chemical agents).

Injection of allergens, from insect bites and stings or drug administration, can introduce allergens directly into the circulation, where they may cause systemwide responses (including anaphylaxis), as well as the local ones of swelling and irritation at the injection site.

Genetic Links

People with allergies are not equally sensitive to all allergens. Some may have severe allergic rhinitis but no food allergies, for instance, or be extremely sensitive to nuts but not to any other food. Allergies may get worse over time. For example, childhood ragweed allergy may progress to year-round dust and pollen allergy. On the other hand, a person may lose allergic sensitivity. Infant or childhood atopic dermatitis disappears in almost all people. More commonly, what seems to be loss of sensitivity is instead a reduced exposure to allergens or an increased tolerance for the same level of symptoms.

While allergy to specific allergens is not inherited, the likelihood of developing some type of allergy seems to be, at least for many people. If neither parent has allergies, the chances of a child developing allergy is approximately 10–20%; if one parent has allergies, it is 30–50%; and if both have allergies, it is 40–75%. One source of this genetic predisposition is in the ability to produce higher levels of IgE in response to allergens. Those who produce more IgE will develop a stronger allergic sensitivity. . . .

Symptoms Vary

Symptoms depend on the specific type of allergic reaction. Allergic rhinitis is characterized by an itchy, runny nose, often with a scratchy or irritated throat due to postnasal drip. Inflammation of the thin membrane covering the eye (allergic conjunctivitis) causes redness, irritation, and increased tearing in the eyes. Asthma causes wheezing, coughing, and shortness of breath. Symptoms of food allergies depend on the tissues most sensitive to the allergen and whether the allergen was spread systemically by the circulatory system. Gastrointestinal symptoms may include swelling and tingling in the lips, tongue, palate or throat; nausea; cramping; diarrhea; and gas. Contact dermatitis is marked by reddened, itchy, weepy skin blisters, and an eczema that is slow to heal. It sometimes has a characteristic man-made pattern, such as a glove allergy with clear demarkation on the hands, wrist, and arms where the gloves are worn, or on the earlobes by wearing earrings.

Whole body or systemic reactions may occur from any type of allergen, but are more common following ingestion or injection of an allergen. Skin reactions include the raised, reddened, and itchy patches called hives that characteristically blanch with pressure and resolve within twenty-four hours. A deeper and more extensive skin reaction, involving more extensive fluid collection and pain, is called angioedema. This usually occurs on the extremities, fingers, toes, and parts of the head, neck, and face. Anaphylaxis is marked by airway constriction, blood pressure drop, widespread tissue swelling, heart rhythm abnormalities, and in some cases, loss of consciousness. Other symptoms may include dizziness, weakness, seizures, coughing, flushing, or cramping. The symptoms may begin within five minutes after exposure to the allergen up to one hour or more later. Mast cells in the tissues and basophils in the blood release mediators that give rise to the clinical symptoms of this IgE-mediated hypersensitivity reaction. Commonly, this is associated with allergies to medications, foods, and insect venoms. In some individuals, anaphylaxis can occur with exercise, plasma exchange, hemodialysis, reaction to insulin, contrast media used in certain types of medical tests, and rarely during the administration of local anesthetics.

Diagnosis by Testing

Allergies can often be diagnosed by a careful medical history, matching the onset of symptoms to the exposure to possible allergens. Allergy is suspected if the symptoms presented are characteristic of an allergic reaction and this occurs repeatedly upon exposure to the suspected allergen. Allergy tests can be used to identify potential allergens, but these must be supported by evidence of allergic responses in the patient's clinical history.

Skin tests are performed by administering a tiny dose of the suspected allergen by pricking, scratching, puncturing or injecting the skin. The allergen is applied to the skin as an aqueous extract, usually on the back, forearms, or top of the thighs. Once in the skin, the allergen may produce a classic immune wheal and flare response (a skin lesion with a raised, white, compressible area surrounded by a red flare). The tests usually begin with prick tests or patch tests that expose the skin to small amounts of allergen to observe the response. A positive reaction will occur on the skin even if the allergen is at levels normally encountered in food or in the airways. Reactions are usually evaluated approximately fifteen minutes after exposure. Intradermal skin tests involved injection of the allergen into the dermis of the skin. These tests are more sensitive and are used for allergies associated with risk of death, such as allergies to antibiotics. . . .

Treatment

Avoiding allergens is the first line of defense to reduce the possibility of an allergic attack. It is helpful to avoid environmental irritants such as tobacco smoke, perfumes, household cleaning agents, paints, glues, air fresheners, and potpourri. Nitrogen dioxide from poorly vented gas stoves, woodburning stoves, and artificial fireplaces has also been linked to poor asthma control. Dust mite control is particularly important in the bedroom areas by use of allergen-impermeable covers on mattress and pillows, frequent washing of bedding in hot water, and removal of items that collect dust such as stuffed toys. Mold growth may be reduced by lowering indoor humidity, repair of house foundations to reduce indoor leaks and seepage, and installing exhaust systems to ventilate areas where steam is generated such as the bathroom or kitchen. Allergic individuals should avoid pet allergens such as saliva, body excretions, pelts, urine, or feces. For those who insist on keeping a pet, restriction of the animal's activity to certain areas of the home may be beneficial.

Complete environmental control is often difficult to accomplish, hence therapeutic interventions may become necessary. A large number of prescription and over-the-counter drugs are available for treatment of immediate hypersensitivity reactions. Most of these work by decreasing the ability of histamine to provoke symptoms. Other drugs counteract the effects of histamine by stimulating other systems or reducing immune responses in general.

Antihistamines block the histamine receptors on nasal tissue, decreasing the effect of histamine released by mast cells. They may be used after symptoms appear, though they may be even more effective when used preventively, before symptoms appear. Antihistamines help reduce sneezing, itching, and rhinorrhea. A wide variety of antihistamines are available.

Hay Fever

American College of Allergy, Asthma, and Immunology

Hay fever, as allergies to pollen are commonly known, has nothing to do with hay or fevers. The technical term for the affliction is allergic rhinitis. In the following selection the American College of Allergy, Asthma, and Immunology (ACAAI) describes the types of so-called hay fever, how it affects the body, and some means of treating it. Surprisingly, the most common response—to change locales—turns out to be one of the least effective. The ACAAI is a professional association of five thousand allergists and immunologists. Established in 1942, the ACAAI strives to improve the quality of patient care in allergy and immunology through research, advocacy, and professional public education.

Allergies, including allergic rhinitis, affect an estimated 40 to 50 million people in the United States. Some allergies may interfere with day-to-day activities or lessen the quality of life. . . .

SOURCE: "Advice From Your Allergist: Rhinitis," ACAAI Online, www.acaai.org. March 27, 2008. Reproduced by permission.

Rhinitis is a term describing the symptoms produced by nasal irritation or inflammation. Symptoms of rhinitis include runny nose, itching, sneezing and stuffy nose due to blockage or congestion. These symptoms are the nose's natural response to inflammation and irritation, and they are often associated with itching of the eyes.

Length of Suffering Varies

Arbitrarily, rhinitis lasting less than six weeks is called acute rhinitis, and persistent symptoms are called chronic rhinitis. Acute rhinitis is usually caused by infections or chemical irritation. Chronic rhinitis may be caused by allergy or a variety of other factors.

The nose normally produces mucus, which traps substances like dust, pollen, pollution, and germs such as bacteria and viruses. Mucus flows from the front of the nose and drains down the back of the throat. When mucus production is excessive, it can flow from the front, as a runny nose, or become noticeable from the back, as post-nasal drip. Nasal mucus, normally a thin, clear liquid, can become thick or colored, perhaps due to dryness, infection or pollution. When post-nasal drip is excessive, thick, or contains irritating substances, cough is the natural response for clearing the throat.

Itching and sneezing are also natural responses to irritation caused by allergic reactions, chemical exposures including cigarette smoke, or temperature changes, infections and other factors.

The nasal tissues congest and decongest periodically. In most people, nasal congestion switches back and forth from side to side of the nose in a cycle several hours long. Some people, especially those with narrow nasal passages, notice this nasal cycle more than others. Strenuous exercise or changes in head position can affect nasal congestion. Severe congestion can result in facial pressure and pain, as well as dark circles under the eyes.

Sinusitis is inflammation or infection of any of the four groups of sinus cavities in the skull, which open into the nasal passages. Sinusitis is not the same as rhinitis, although the two may be associated and their symptoms may be similar. The terms "sinus trouble" or "sinus congestion" are sometimes wrongly used to mean congestion of the nasal passage itself. Most cases of nasal congestion, though, are not associated with sinusitis.

Hay Fever's Origins

Known to most people as hay fever, allergic rhinitis is a very common medical problem affecting more than 15 percent of the population, both adults and children.

Allergic rhinitis takes two different forms: seasonal and perennial. Symptoms of seasonal allergic rhinitis occur in spring, summer and/or early fall and are usually caused by allergic sensitivity to pollens from trees, grasses or weeds, or to airborne mold spores. Other people experience symptoms year-round, a condition called "perennial allergic rhinitis." It's generally caused by sensitivity to house dust mites, animal dander and/or mold spores. Underlying or hidden food allergies are sometimes a cause of perennial nasal symptoms.

Some people may experience both types of rhinitis, with perennial symptoms worsening during specific pollen seasons. As will be discussed later, there are also other causes for rhinitis.

When a sensitive person inhales an allergen (allergy-causing substance) like ragweed pollen, the body's immune system reacts abnormally with the allergen. The allergen binds to allergic antibodies (immunoglobulin E [IgE]) that are attached to cells that produce histamine and other chemicals. The pollen "triggers" these cells in the nasal membranes, causing them to release histamine and the other chemicals. Histamine dilates the small blood vessels of the nose and fluids leak out into the surrounding tissues, causing runny noses, watery eyes, itching, swelling and other allergy symptoms.

Antibodies circulate in the blood stream, but localize in the tissues of the nose and in the skin. This makes it possible to show the presence of these antibodies by skin testing, or less commonly, by a special IgE allergy blood test. A positive skin test mirrors the type of reaction going on in the nose.

"Hay fever" is a turn-of-the-century term that has come to describe the symptoms of allergic rhinitis, especially when it occurs in the late summer. However, the symptoms are not caused by hay (ragweed is one of the

Hay fever, or allergic rhinitis, is not caused by hay but by pollen. (© Andrew Fox/Alamy)

main culprits) and are not accompanied by fever. So, the term "allergic rhinitis" is more accurate. Similarly, springtime symptoms are sometimes called "rose fever," but it's just coincidental that roses are in full-bloom during the grass-pollinating season. Roses and other sweet-smelling, showy flowers rely on bees, not the wind, for pollination, so not much of their pollen gets into the air to cause allergies.

Moving Is No Cure

A common question from allergic rhinitis sufferers is: Can I move someplace where my allergies will go away?

Some allergens are tough to escape. Ragweed, which affects 75 percent of allergic rhinitis sufferers, blankets most of the United States. Less ragweed is found in a band along the West Coast, the southern-most tip of Florida and northern Maine, but it is still present. Even parts of Alaska and Hawaii have a little ragweed.

Allergist-immunologists seldom recommend moving to another locale as a cure for allergies. A move may be of questionable value because a person may escape one allergy to ragweed, for example, only to develop sensitivity to grasses or other allergens in the new location. Since moving can have a disrupting effect on a family financially and emotionally, relocation should be considered only in an extreme situation and only after consultation with an allergist-immunologist. . . .

Diagnosis and Treatment

Sometimes several conditions can coexist in the same person. In a single individual, allergic rhinitis could be complicated by vasomotor [chronic nonallergenic] rhinitis, septal deviation (curvature of the bone separating the two sides of the nose) or nasal polyps. Use of spray decongestants for chronic sinusitis, septal deviation or vasomotor rhinitis may cause rhinitis medicamentosa. Any of these conditions will be made worse by catching a cold. Nasal symptoms caused by more than one problem can be difficult to treat, often requiring the cooperation of an allergist-immunologist and an otolaryngologist (ear, nose and throat specialist).

Your allergist-immunologist may begin by taking a detailed history, looking for clues in your lifestyle that will help pinpoint the cause of your symptoms. You'll be asked about your work and home environments, your eating habits, your family's medical history, the frequency and severity of your symptoms, and miscellaneous matters, such as if you have pets. Then, you may require some tests. Your allergist-immunologist may employ skin testing, in which small amounts of suspected allergens are introduced into the skin. Skin-testing is the easiest, most sensitive and generally least expensive way of making the diagnosis. Another advantage is that results are available immediately. In rare cases, it also may be necessary to do a special IgE allergy blood test for specific allergens.

FAST FACT

According to the National Center for Health Statistics, in 2006, 6.8 million children in the United States suffered from hay fever.

When no specific cure is available, options are ignoring your symptoms, avoiding or decreasing exposure to irritants or allergens to the extent practical, and taking medications for symptom relief.

Once allergic rhinitis is diagnosed, treatment options include avoidance, medication and immunotherapy (allergy shots).

Avoidance—A single ragweed plant may release one million pollen grains in just one day. The pollen from ragweed, grasses and trees is so small and buoyant that the wind may carry it miles from its source. Mold spores, which grow outdoors in fields and on dead leaves, also are everywhere and may outnumber pollen grains in the air even when the pollen season is at its worst.

While it's difficult to escape pollen and molds, here are some ways to lessen exposure.

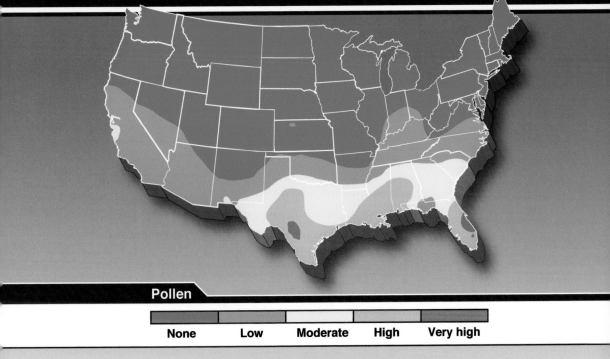

Pollen Density Map

Maps like this are updated daily to show pollen count.

Pollen

| None | Low | Moderate | High | Very high |

Taken from: www.allaboutvision.com/pollen, September 29, 2008.

- Keep windows closed and use air-conditioning in the summer, if possible. A HEPA (High Efficiency Particulate Air) filter or an electrostatic precipitator may help clean pollen and mold from the indoor air. Automobile air conditioners help, too.

- Don't hang clothing outdoors to dry. Pollen may cling to towels and sheets.

- The outdoor air is most heavily saturated with pollen and mold between 5 and 10 A.M., so early morning is a good time to limit outdoor activities.

- Wear a dust mask when mowing the lawn, raking leaves or gardening, and take appropriate medication beforehand.

Medication—When avoidance measures don't control symptoms, medication may be the answer. Antihistamines and decongestants are the most commonly used medications for allergic rhinitis. Other medications, such as cromolyn (Nasalcrom), inhibit the release of chemicals that cause allergic reactions. Nasal corticosteroid sprays reduce the inflammation from the allergic trigger. Medications help to alleviate nasal congestion, runny nose, sneezing and itching. They are available in many forms, including tablets, nasal sprays, eye drops and liquids. Some medications may cause side effects, so its best to consult your allergist-immunologist if there's a problem.

Immunotherapy—Allergen immunotherapy, known as "allergy shots," may be recommended for persons who don't respond well to treatment with medications, experience side-effects from medications or have allergen exposure that is unavoidable. Immunotherapy can be very effective in controlling allergic symptoms. Allergy injections are usually given at variable intervals over a period of three to five years.

An immunotherapy treatment program consists of injections of a diluted allergy extract, administered frequently in increasing doses until a maintenance dose is reached. Then, the injection schedule is changed so that the same dose is given with longer intervals between injections. Immunotherapy helps the body build resistance to the effects of the allergen, reduces the intensity of symptoms caused by allergen exposure, and sometimes can actually make skin test reactions disappear. As resistance develops, symptoms should improve, but the improvement from immunotherapy will take several months to occur. Immunotherapy does not help the symptoms produced by non-allergic rhinitis.

There are many ways of treating allergies, and each person's treatment must be individualized based on the frequency, severity and duration of symptoms and on the degree or allergic sensitivity.

Food Allergies

Janice M. Vickerstaff Joneja

Food provides the fuel that we need to live on, but sometimes a person's body mistakes food for a harmful invader. In that case a food allergy may develop. In the following selection, Janice M. Vickerstaff Joneja explains the unique properties of food allergies and how they differ from food sensitivities. The severity of symptoms of food allergies varies widely, she indicates, as do the kinds of food that trigger them. What all food allergies have in common is that the body's immune system sets in motion a cascade of inappropriate defensive reactions that end up hurting the individual—sometimes with fatal consequences. Canadian dietician Janice M. Vickerstaff Joneja is the author of several books on food allergies. She holds a doctorate in her field and is a registered dietician.

I n popular literature, it has become convenient for all adverse reactions that result from eating to be labeled food allergy. The word allergy is commonly misused,

SOURCE: Janice M. Vickerstaff Joneja, "Food Allergies: The Immune Response," *Today's Dietician*, July 2007. Reprinted with the permission of *Today's Dietitian*. Copyright © 2007 Great Valley Publishing Co.

even by health professionals who do not understand the complex mechanisms of an allergic reaction. This article will explain those mechanisms and help dietetic professionals understand how and why the miserable symptoms we call food allergy, food intolerance, food sensitivity, or adverse reactions to foods occur.

The symptoms of an allergic reaction are caused by biologically active chemicals produced by the immune system in its attempt to protect the body from a foreign invader. Our immune system is designed to protect us from anything that may cause disease. Usually, this is a microorganism such as a virus, bacterium, or other pathogen.

However, the immune system of an allergic (atopic) person attempts to "protect" the body from harmless substances such as pollens, animal dander, dust mites, mold spores, and components of certain foods. The question that has always puzzled doctors and scientists is: What causes the immune system of one individual to fight a harmless substance while another's system recognizes the same materials as innocuous?

Food Is Not at Fault

Although we do not know the entire answer to that question, we know that food itself is incapable of causing any disease in the way that viruses, bacteria, and cancer cells can; there are no "bad foods." Rather, it is the body's response to components of a food that causes symptoms. The explanation for why one person's body responds to food by developing distressing symptoms and another's uses the same food for comfort and nurture lies in the process of recognizing what is safe and what may be harmful to the body. Several factors are involved, including the following:

- the individual's inherited genetic makeup;
- the circumstances under which the food was first encountered;

Allergic Reactions to Food: Common Symptoms

Experts estimate that 40 to 50 million Americans have various allergies, but only 1 to 2 percent of adults are allergic to foods. Of children under the age of six, 2 to 5 percent have food allergies.

Symptoms

Symptoms of an allergic reaction to food typically appear within a few minutes to a few hours after a person has eaten an offending food.

Tingling sensation in the mouth
Swelling of the tongue and throat
Difficulty breathing
Hives or eczema
Vomiting
Abdominal cramps
Diarrhea
Drop in blood pressure
Loss of consciousness and death

Taken from: U.S. Food and Drug Administration. www.fda.gov/FDAC/features/2001/401_food.html./ American College of Allergy, Asthma, and Immunology. www.acaai.org/public/advice/foods.htm.

- the type of microorganisms that live within the digestive tract;
- other diseases present at the same time;
- oral medications; and
- other immunological factors that we are only beginning to understand.

Moreover, food sensitivity is unlike any other disease entity in that it has many different causes since any food is capable of triggering an allergy in a person who has been sensitized to it or who lacks the systems required to process it adequately when it enters the body. The same food may be absolutely safe for others.

Furthermore, food allergy can result in different symptoms in diverse organ systems. For example, one person may develop skin symptoms such as eczema or hives; another may have digestive tract symptoms such as stomachache, diarrhea, nausea, or vomiting; and another may develop symptoms in the lungs such as asthma or in the upper respiratory tract such as a stuffy, runny nose or earache. Sometimes, all body systems are involved (anaphylaxis). And all these varied reactions may come from eating the same food, such as peanuts or shellfish. Each allergic individual differs in the way his or her immune system responds to food and which foods it responds to.

Allergy Versus Intolerance

For many years, the nomenclature for food allergy and other adverse reactions to food was based on the directives of the American Academy of Allergy, Asthma & Immunology (AAAAI) and the National Institute of Allergy and Infectious Diseases (part of the National Institutes of Health [NIH]). They define an adverse food reaction as any untoward reaction after the ingestion of a food, which can include food allergy or food intolerance. The difference is that a food allergy is the result of an abnormal immunologic response after ingestion of a food and a food intolerance is the result of nonimmunological mechanisms.

However, as research has progressed, further distinctions have been made. The most recent (2001) definitions from the European Academy of Allergology and Clinical Immunology (EAACI) define allergy as a hypersensitivity reaction initiated by immunologic mechanisms. Thus, when immunologic mechanisms have been demonstrated, the appropriate term is food allergy. If the role of immunoglobulin (Ig) E is highlighted, the correct term is IgE-mediated food allergy. All other reactions, previously referred to as food intolerance, should be referred to as nonallergic food hypersensitivity. Any adverse reaction to food should be called food hypersensitivity.

Severe, generalized allergic reactions to food can be classified as anaphylaxis, a severe, life-threatening, generalized, or systemic hypersensitivity reaction. Atopy is a personal or familial tendency to produce IgE antibodies in response to low doses of allergens, usually proteins, and to develop typical symptoms such as asthma, rhinoconjunctivitis (hay fever), or eczema/dermatitis. . . .

The Allergic Reaction

A food allergy is a response of the immune system to an antigen in a food that it recognizes as "foreign." (Note: An antigen is a protein, glycoprotein, or a molecule linked to a protein that elicits a response of the immune system.) Antigens that trigger an allergic reaction are called allergens. When an allergen enters the body of a person at risk for allergy, an extremely complex series of events is set in motion that will result in the release of chemicals (called inflammatory mediators) that act on body tissues to cause the symptoms of allergy. All immunological processes involve white blood cells (leukocytes) and the different types of chemicals they produce.

> **FAST FACT**
>
> Contrary to popular myth, no one is allergic to sugar. The American Academy of Family Physicians states that only foods containing proteins are allergenic.

The first stage of the immunological response involves recognition of the invading antigen. All foods contain numerous antigens. Not all antigens are allergens, but all allergens are antigens.

When an antigen enters the body, white blood cells called lymphocytes are activated to recognize and respond to anything foreign. We can visualize lymphocytes as the sentinels of the immune system. There are two different types of lymphocytes in blood: T cells and B cells.

When a rash on the skin appears, an allergic reaction has occurred due to an antigen becoming an allergen. (© Bubbles Photolibrary/Alamy)

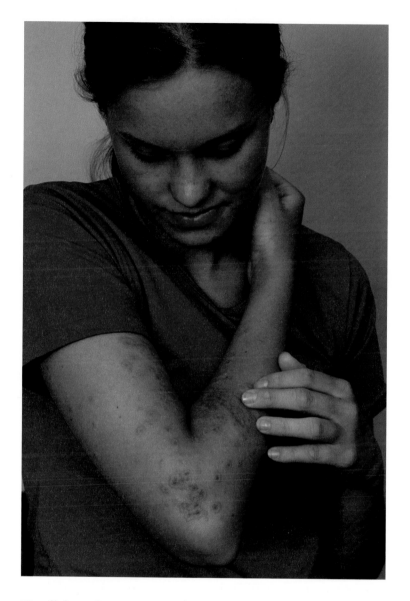

T-cell lymphocytes are the ultimate "gatekeepers" and controllers of the immune system.

Certain types of T cells, called helper T cells (Th cells), are responsible for identifying foreign materials that enter the body through any route, such as the mouth, nose, and skin. They initiate and direct the subsequent activities of the immune system if the foreign material is deemed a threat. T cells exert their control of the whole immune response by means of a number of different types of "messenger chemicals" called cytokines. The response of T-helper cells in allergic and nonallergic individuals is different. The two types of responses have been designated Th2 and Th1 response, respectively. Different cytokines are released in each response and control the way the body reacts to the foreign material. . . .

Symptoms such as fever, aching muscles, fatigue, and general malaise that are typical of an infection such as the flu are the result of the body's response to cytokines and other inflammatory mediators produced during this battle between the immune system and the foreign invader. In an allergic reaction, a similar battle is engaged, but this time, it is between the immune system and a nonthreatening invader such as a food. . . .

Simply stated, the Th1 response protects the body from disease, and IgG are the antibodies responsible for the ultimate destruction of the invader. The Th2 response results in allergies, and IgE antibodies are responsible for the release of inflammatory mediators that cause the symptoms of the allergy. . . .

A single exposure to an allergen rarely results in the release of inflammatory mediators and is usually symptom-free. However, once the allergen-specific T and B cells have been produced, memory cells remain, which respond immediately when the same allergen enters the body on a subsequent occasion. Thus, every exposure after the first will result in the immediate production of antibodies specific to the triggering antigen or allergen), and the amount of antibodies in circulation will increase with each exposure.

Pet Allergies

Asthma and Allergy Foundation of America

People may love their pets, but sometimes their bodies reject them. In the following selection the Asthma and Allergy Foundation of America (AAFA) explains how pet allergies come about and what people can do about them. With more than 100 million pets in America, it is difficult for anyone to avoid contact. However, people with severe allergies to pets have to take steps to protect themselves. Contrary to popular belief, it is not the fur of pets like cats and dogs that triggers an allergic reaction. Rather, the AAFA explains, it is dander, which bears allergenic proteins. Since dander consists of invisible, airborne flakes, living with a dog or cat can be extremely difficult for an allergy sufferer. The Asthma and Allergy Foundation of America is a nonprofit organization that provides practical information, community-based services, and support for people with asthma and allergies. Founded in 1953, it is the oldest asthma and allergy patient organization in the world.

SOURCE: "Pet Allergies," aafa.org, 2005. Copyright © 2005 The Asthma and Allergy Foundation of America (AAFA). Reproduced by permission. For more information, visit www.aafa.org.

Six out of 10 people in the United States come in contact with cats or dogs. The total pet population is more than 100 million, or about four pets for every 10 people.

Allergies to pets with fur or feathers are common, especially among people who have other allergies or asthma. From 15 percent to 30 percent of people with allergies have allergic reactions to cats and dogs.

People with dog allergies may be allergic to all dogs or to only some breeds. Cat allergies are about twice as common as dog allergies.

The job of immune system cells is to find foreign substances such as viruses and bacteria and get rid of them. Normally, this response protects us from dangerous diseases. People with pet allergies have supersensitive immune systems that react to harmless proteins in the pet's dander (dead skin that is shed), saliva or urine. These proteins are called allergens.

Pet Populations Are Growing Rapidly

Surveys show that over half of all American households now have at least one cat or dog sharing the home. The pet dog population is over 67 million, and the pet cat population is well over 83 million.

	2002	2007
Dogs	60,730,000	67,085,100
Cats	76,810,000	83,884,300

Taken from: Pet Food Institute. www.petfoodinstitute.org/reference_pet_data.cfm.
Data source: Euromonitor International.

Dogs and cats secrete fluids and shed dander that contain the allergens. They collect on fur and other surfaces. The allergens will not lose their strength for a long time, sometimes for several months. They appear to be sticky and adhere to walls, clothing and other surfaces.

Pet hair is not an allergen. It can collect dander, though. It also harbors other allergens like dust and pollen.

FAST FACT

Cat allergies are twice as common as dog allergies.

Cat and dog allergens are everywhere. Pet dander is even in homes never occupied by these animals because it is carried on people's clothing. The allergens get in the air with petting, grooming or stirring the air where the allergens have settled. Once airborne, the particles can stay suspended in the air for long periods of time.

Range of Symptoms

Reactions to cat and dog allergens that land on the membranes that line eyes and nose include swelling and itching of the membranes, stuffy nose and inflamed eyes. A pet scratch or lick can cause the skin area to become red.

If allergen levels are low or sensitivity is minor, symptoms may not appear until after several days of contact with the pet.

Many airborne particles are small enough to get into the lungs. When inhaled, the allergens combine with antibodies. This can cause severe breathing problems—coughing, wheezing and shortness of breath—in highly sensitive people within 15 to 30 minutes. Sometimes highly sensitive people also get an intense rash on the face, neck and upper chest.

For about 20 percent to 30 percent of people with asthma, cat contact can trigger a severe asthma attack. Cat allergies also can lead to chronic asthma.

If a pet allergy is suspected, the doctor may diagnose it by taking a medical history and testing the blood of the patient. Some people are so attached to their pets that they will deny the pets could cause their symptoms. In these cases, the patient is removed from the animal's environment to see if symptoms go away. It does not help to remove the dog or cat. Allergens still in the area can cause symptoms months after the animal is gone.

To diagnose cat-induced asthma, the patient must have both of the following:

- Asthma symptoms when exposed to cat or cat allergen.
- An allergic reaction to a skin test or to a blood test called RAST (radioallergosorbent test). To make sure the diagnosis is correct, the doctor will watch what happens when a cat is added then removed from the patient's environment several times.

Choices After Diagnosis

The best treatment is to avoid contact with cats or dogs or their dander. Keep the pets out of the house, and avoid visiting people with pets. Avoiding cats and dogs may give you enough relief that you will not need medication.

Keeping the pet outdoors will help, but will not rid the house of pet allergens. Another option is to have pets that do not have fur or feathers. Fish, snakes or turtles are some choices.

To test the effect of household pets on your quality of life, remove them from your home for at least two months and clean thoroughly every week. After two months, if you still want pets, bring a pet into the house. Measure the change in your symptoms, then decide if the change in your symptoms is worth keeping the pet.

Bedroom Ban

If you decide to keep a pet, bar it from the bedroom. You spend from one-third to one-half of your time there. Keep the bedroom door closed and clean the bedroom aggressively:

• Because animal allergens are sticky, you must remove the animal's favorite furniture, remove wall-to-wall carpet and scrub the walls and woodwork. Keep surfaces throughout the home clean and uncluttered. Bare floors and walls are best.

People are likely to be twice as susceptible to cat allergies as to dog allergies.
(© Carlos Davila/Alamy)

- If you must have carpet, select ones with a low pile and steam clean them frequently. Better yet, use throw rugs that can be washed in hot water.
- Wear a dust mask to vacuum. Vacuum cleaners stir up allergens that have settled on carpet and make allergies worse. Use a vacuum with a HEPA (high efficiency particulate air) filter if possible.
- Forced-air heating and air-conditioning can spread allergens through the house. Cover bedroom vents with dense filtering material like cheesecloth.
- Adding an air cleaner with a HEPA filter to central heating and air conditioning can help remove pet allergens from the air. The air cleaner should be used at least four hours per day. Another type of air cleaner that has an electrostatic filter will remove particles the size of animal allergens from the air. No air cleaner or filter will remove allergens stuck to surfaces, though.
- Washing the pet every week may reduce airborne allergens, but is of questionable value in reducing a person's symptoms.
- Have someone without a pet allergy brush the pet outside to remove dander as well as clean the litter box or cage.

Dust Mites: Allergens Hiding in Your Bed

William F. Lyon

One of the most common causes of allergies in the home is something most people have never seen. Dust mites are tiny, spiderlike creatures that infest bedding. In the following selection, insect expert William F. Lyon discusses the dimensions of the problem and what can be done about it. In a typical bed, he said, millions of house dust mites may live in the pillows and mattress. Invisible to the eye and reclusive by nature, they live on the flakes of dead skin that people constantly shed. The mites excrete feces that eventually become airborne particles of dust. These are the source of allergy for people allergic to dust mites. Although complete eradication is very difficult to achieve, Lyon says that dust mite populations can be suppressed by reducing the humidity and putting special covers over pillows. He also recommends air purifying systems for some people. William F. Lyon is professor emeritus of entomology at Ohio State University.

One of the most strongly allergenic materials found indoors is house dust, often heavily contaminated with the fecal pellets and cast skins of house dust

SOURCE: William F. Lyon, "House Dust Mites," *Ohio State University Extension Fact Sheet*. Reproduced by permission.

mites. Estimates are that dust mites may be a factor in 50 to 80 percent of asthmatics, as well as in countless cases of eczema, hay fever and other allergic ailments. Common causes of allergy include house dust mites, cat dander, cockroach droppings and grass pollen. Symptoms are usually respiratory in nature (sneezing, itching, watery eyes, wheezing, etc.), usually not a rash. However, there are reports of a red rash around the neck. Other allergic reactions may include headaches, fatigue and depression.

The wheeze-inducing proteins are digestive juices from the mite gut which are quite potent. An exposure to the mites in the first, crucial year of life can trigger a lifelong

One of the most common causes of allergies in the home is the lowly dust mite, shown here under a microscope. (Dr. Darlyne A. Marawski/ National Geographic/ Getty Images)

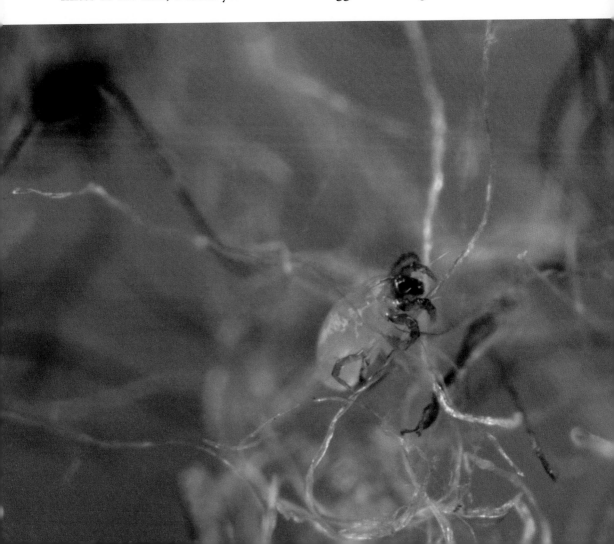

allergy. There is no cure, only prevention. One must control house dust mite levels.

Millions of Mites

Beds are a prime habitat (where 1/3 of [a person's] life occurs). A typical used mattress may have anywhere from 100,000 to 10 million mites inside. (Ten percent of the weight of a two year old pillow can be composed of dead mites and their droppings.) Mites prefer warm, moist surroundings such as the inside of a mattress when someone is on it. A favorite food is dander (both human and animal skin flakes). Humans shed about 1/5 ounce of dander (dead skin) each week. About 80 percent of the material seen floating in a sunbeam is actually skin flakes. Also, bedroom carpeting and household upholstery support high mite populations.

House dust mites, due to their very small size (250 to 300 microns in length) and translucent bodies, are not visible to the unaided eye. For accurate identification, one needs at least 10X magnification. The adult mite's cuticle (covering) has simple striations that can be seen from both the dorsal (top) view and from the ventral (bottom) view. The ventral view of the house dust mite reveals long setae (hairs) extending from the outer margins of the body and shorter setae on the rest of the body. Through the microscope, one will see many oval-shaped mites scuttling around and over one another. There are eight hairy legs, no eyes, no antennae, a mouthpart group in front of the body (resembles head) and a tough, translucent shell, giving a fearsome appearance.

A Mite's Life

Adult females lay . . . 40 to 80 eggs singly or in small groups of three to five. After eggs hatch, a six-legged larva emerges. After the first molt, an eight-legged nymph appears. After two nymphal stages occur, an eight-legged adult emerges. The life cycle from egg to adult is about one month with the adult living an additional one to three months.

The diet is varied, with the primary food source consisting of dander (skin scales) from humans and animals. However, needed nutrients can be provided from fish food flakes, pet food, fungi, cereals, crumbs, etc. Many mite species live in bird's nests, in barns, among stored grain, straw, etc.

House dust mites are cosmopolitan in distribution with much of the research previously done in Europe.

One of the major limiting factors in mite survival and population development is the availability of water. . . . Highest mite densities occur in the humid summer months and lowest in drier winter periods. Dust mite populations are highest in humid regions and lowest in areas of high altitude and/or dry climates. . . .

Countermeasures

House dust mite presence is often suspected before they are actually seen and accurately identified. Requests for control often come from individuals who have been diagnosed by medical personnel as allergic to the house dust mite or the allergens produced. . . .

Recommendations focus on "dust control." One must reduce the concentration of dust borne allergens in the living environment by controlling both allergen production and the dust which serves to transport it. For the bedroom environment:

1. Replace feather and down pillows with those having synthetic fillings.
2. Enclose the mattress top and sides with a plastic cover, thoroughly vacuuming mattress, pillows and the base of the bed.
3. Daily damp dust the plastic mattress cover.
4. Weekly change and wash pillowcases, sheets, and under blankets, and vacuum the bed base and around the covered mattress.

The Mite Population Rises with Humidity

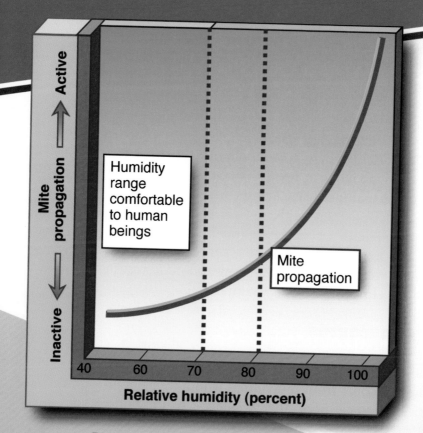

Taken from: Inax, "Reducing Mold and Mites." www.inax-ecocarat.com.

5. Replace woolen blankets with nylon or cotton cellulose ones.

6. Frequently wash all bedding (blankets, mattress pads and comforters) in hot water (130 degrees F [Fahrenheit] weekly). Also wash curtains.

7. Remove carpet and replace with wood, tile, linoleum, or vinyl floor covering. (If you have carpet, vacuum every day.)

8. Mattresses covered with "fitted sheets" help prevent the accumulation of human skin scales on the surface (an alternate to encasing mattresses and box springs in non-allergenic, impermeable, plastic covers).

The application of frequent vacuuming as a dust control measure is more likely to aggravate allergic asthmatic conditions because conventional vacuums are very inefficient. Dust collection by conventional vacuums results in a significant increase in air borne dust concentrations. Vacuuming is best accomplished by cleaners that entrain dust into a liquid medium such as water (rather than a dust bag), which reduces the suspension and dissemination of allergenic dust particles in the air. . . .

Various types of air purifiers can be attached to the central air return to decrease irritants. Most filters remove 50 to 70 percent of material. HEPA filters will remove up to 99 percent of the material. Indoor air quality is very important. (One needs to bring in fresh outside air rather than recirculating dirty air.) Some filters need to be changed monthly.

Some feel it is important to focus on decreasing indoor humidity, especially during the winter period to reduce dust mite populations. One might forsake humidifier use during winter periods, use of dehumidifiers during high-humidity periods, or use of central air conditioning. Effective control of mites would require the maintenance of relative humidities below 50 percent (mites thrive in humid conditions).

Homes that have their air conditioners on constantly have lower mite counts than non-air-conditioned homes.

> **FAST FACT**
>
> Experts say that children's stuffed toys can be reservoirs for dust mites. They recommend washing toys in hot water or, if that is not possible, placing them in a freezer for at least twenty-four hours.

When Allergies Strike, Anaphylaxis May Swiftly Follow

David C. Dugdale, Stuart I. Henochowicz, David Zieve

How a person's body reacts to an allergy can vary widely. When the reaction to an allergy is severe and quite sudden, it is referred to as anaphylaxis. The word is derived from the Greek meaning "counter-productive," which is exactly what happens within the body when ana-phylaxis occurs. According to the following selection from MedlinePlus, anaphylaxis can be life threatening. MedlinePlus brings together authoritative information from the National Institutes of Health and other government agencies and health-related organizations.

A naphylaxis is a life-threatening type of allergic reaction.

Anaphylaxis is a severe, whole-body allergic reaction. After being exposed to a substance like bee sting venom, the person's immune system becomes sensitized

SOURCE: David C. Dugdale, Stuart I. Henochowicz, David Zieve, "Medical Encyclopedia: Anaphylaxis," MedlinePlus, the U.S. National Library of Medicine and the National Institutes of Health, April 28, 2008. www.nlm.nih.gov/medlineplus/ency/article/000844.htm.

to that allergen. On a later exposure, an allergic reaction may occur. This reaction is sudden, severe, and involves the whole body.

Tissues in different parts of the body release histamine and other substances. This causes the airways to tighten and leads to other symptoms.

Some drugs (polymyxin, morphine, x-ray dye, and others) may cause an anaphylactic-like reaction (anaphylactoid reaction) when people are first exposed to them. This is usually due to a toxic reaction, rather than the immune system response that occurs with "true" anaphylaxis.

The symptoms, risk for complications without treatment, and treatment are the same, however, for both types of reactions.

Anaphylaxis can occur in response to any allergen. Common causes include: Drug allergies, food allergies, [or] insect bites/stings.

Potential Allergy Triggers in the Classroom

- Dust mites
- Chalk dust
- Pollen and molds
- Exercise
- Insect stings
- Animal dander from class pets or pet hair on students' clothing
- Pest allergens

Taken from: "Avoiding Allergies and Asthma in the Classroom: Tips from the AAAAI," PR Newswire, August 22, 2007.

Pollens and other inhaled allergens rarely cause anaphylaxis. Some people have an anaphylactic reaction with no known cause.

Anaphylaxis rarely occurs. However, it is life-threatening and can occur at any time. Risks include past history of any type of allergic reaction.

Symptoms develop rapidly, often within seconds or minutes. They may include the following:

- Abdominal pain or cramping
- Abnormal (high-pitched) breathing sounds
- Anxiety
- Confusion
- Cough
- Diarrhea
- Difficulty breathing
- Fainting, light-headedness, dizziness
- Hives, itchiness
- Nasal congestion
- Nausea, vomiting
- Sensation of feeling the heart beat (palpitations)
- Skin redness
- Slurred speech
- Wheezing

Treatment

Anaphylaxis is an emergency condition requiring immediate professional medical attention. Call 911 immediately.

Check the ABC's (airway, breathing, and circulation from Basic Life Support) in all suspected anaphylactic reactions.

CPR should be started, if needed. People with known severe allergic reactions may carry an Epi-Pen or other allergy kit, and should be helped if necessary.

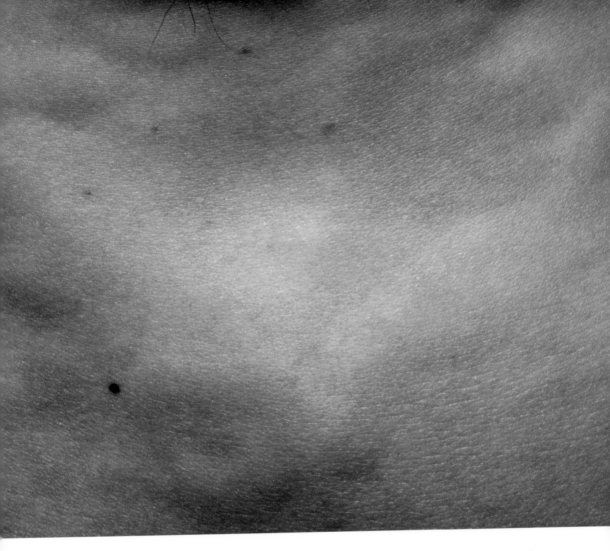

Paramedics or physicians may place a tube through the nose or mouth into the airway (endotracheal intubation) or perform emergency surgery to place a tube directly into the trachea (tracheostomy or cricothyrotomy).

Epinephrine should be given by injection in the thigh muscle right away. This opens the airways and raises the blood pressure by tightening blood vessels.

Treatment for shock includes fluids through a vein (intravenous) and medications that support the actions of the heart and circulatory system.

The person may receive antihistamines such as di-phenhydramine, and corticosteroids such as prednisone

Symptomatic of anaphylaxis is urticaria, a generalized itching, swelling, and redness of the skin. (© Medical-on-line/Alamy)

to further reduce symptoms (after lifesaving measures and epinephrine are administered).

Outlook (Prognosis)

Anaphylaxis is a severe disorder that can be life threatening without prompt treatment. However, symptoms usually get better with the right therapy, so it is important to act right away.

Possible Complications

- Airway blockage
- Cardiac arrest (no effective heartbeat)
- Respiratory arrest (no breathing)
- Shock

Call 911 if you develop severe symptoms of anaphylaxis. If you are with another person, he or she may take you to the nearest emergency room.

Prevention

Avoid known allergens. Any person experiencing an allergic reaction should be monitored, although monitoring may be done at home in mild cases.

Occasionally, people who have a history of drug allergies may safely be given the medication they are allergic to after being pretreated with corticosteroids (prednisone) and antihistamines (diphenhydramine).

People who have a history of allergy to insect bites/stings should carry (and use) an emergency kit containing injectable epinephrine and chewable antihistamine. They should also wear a Medic-Alert or similar bracelet/necklace stating their allergy.

FAST FACT

Nearly 20 percent of Americans suffer from allergies.

CHAPTER 2

Controversies About Allergies

People with Allergies May Be Able to Keep Specially Bred Cats

Rachel Pepling

Cats are the most common pet in America, and they are also the most common source of pet allergies. In the following selection science writer Rachel Pepling examines the claims of one company to have bred a cat that allergy sufferers can live with. The breed of cat, whose exact lineage is a company secret, supposedly lacks a protein thought to be responsible for cat allergies. Only a few hundred of the breed are available, Pepling reports, and each one costs thousands of dollars. Another company is attempting the same feat via genetic engineering, she reports. If these approaches succeed, they could represent a major breakthrough in pet allergies, but as yet no one knows whether the cats in question will suffer harm. Rachel Pepling is an online editor of the journal Chemical & Engineering News.

Photo on previous page. Research has shown that people are more susceptible to cat allergies than originally thought. (© Phototake, Inc./Alamy)

The world's first hypoallergenic cats may soon be curling up and purring in the laps of allergy sufferers, a U.S. company announced [in June 2006].

SOURCE: Rachel Pepling, "Hypoallergenic Cats for Sale, U.S. Firm Announces," *National Geographic News*, June 9, 2006. Reproduced by permission.

Allerca, Inc., a biotechnology firm in San Diego, California, is now taking orders for its Allerca Gene Divergence (GD) kittens.

The cats are not transgenic animals—their genes have not been altered to make them less of an allergy risk. Instead Allerca officials say they searched for natural variations in the cat gene that controls allergy-inducing properties and then bred cats with the desired trait.

Leslie Lyons, an assistant professor in the school of veterinary medicine at the University of California, Davis [UC Davis], specializes in research on domestic cat genetics and is not involved with Allerca's work. "People breed cats all the time, so why not a company who has used empirical data to identify hypoallergenic cats?" Lyons said. "Siberian cats have been touted by breeders as being hypoallergenic for a long time," she said.

If Allerca used Siberians—or another low-allergen breed found through genetic screening—Lyons thinks a hypoallergenic breed could be developed in as few as "one to two crosses."

Secret Breeding Program

Megan Young, Allerca's CEO [chief executive officer], said that the firm has simply "taken selective breeding to the next level." Allerca officials are closely guarding their scientific data, and independent parties have yet to publicly verify the cats' hypoallergenic status.

But Young says human-exposure trials conducted by Allerca and an independent lab revealed that known cat-allergy sufferers ranging from mildly to highly allergic showed no signs of reaction when in contact with the newly bred cats. She also notes that Allerca [planned] to submit its findings for publication in a peer-reviewed journal in early 2007.

Approximately 10 million people in the U.S. are allergic to cats, according to the nonprofit Asthma and Allergy Foundation of America. Cat allergens can trigger

Allerca, Inc. of San Diego, California, has succeeded in breeding a hypoallergenic cat, free of allergens. (© Frances Roberts/Alamy)

severe asthma attacks for 20 to 30 percent of asthma sufferers and exposure can lead to chronic asthma.

Protein Provokes Allergies

Contrary to popular belief, people are not allergic to a cat's fur or dander. The sneezing, wheezing, and itching are brought on by Fel d 1, a protein excreted in feline saliva and skin glands.

Even a hairless breed can trigger an allergic reaction. Cats—notorious self-groomers—transfer the allergy-inducing protein to their skin and fur while licking themselves.

According to Young, Allerca researchers used genetic sequencing to search for natural variations in the genetic code of the Fel d 1 protein. They then selectively bred cats to express the protein at a lower molecular weight, reducing the likelihood of an allergic reaction.

Allerca's low-allergen felines, expected to arrive in homes next spring [2007], carry a price tag that could send some pet lovers into shock. The firm currently charges $3,950 (U.S.) per cat, plus nearly $1,000 for processing and transportation.

The steep cost includes pet insurance, vaccines, a microchip identifier, spaying or neutering, nail caps, and a starter kit. Kittens will be delivered via private jet courier to pre-selected veterinary offices where owners can pick them up.

Because building up a breeding pool takes time, Young projects that Allerca will only have 400 to 500 cats available [in 2007].

As a safety precaution, Young says the kittens will be tested for their Fel d 1 levels before they are delivered. Owners and their homes must also undergo FDA-approved [Food and Drug Administration] allergy tests to create a baseline for any preexisting allergens. Should an individual exceed the threshold level for tolerating the new cats' low levels of allergens, Allerca will strongly suggest the owner not claim the cat and will refund the purchase price.

Another Approach

A Denver, Colorado–based firm, Felix Pets, is trying to produce hypoallergenic cats using a different technique: developing a hypoallergenic cat via direct cellular modification.

In theory, while a developing kitten is still a single cell, its DNA can be modified to remove or suppress the gene that produces the allergen protein, Felix Pets' president David Avner explains. The modified cell would then be implanted into a surrogate mother cat to finish developing into an allergen-free kitten.

Avner says gene modification has an advantage over selective breeding in that modification takes less time to produce a cat consistently free of the allergen protein. "To breed out the allergen could take decades," he said.

Avner says he expects to have transgenic allergen-free cats ready for the market by 2008. While kittens will be "expensive" initially, Avner said, he hopes to eventually sell them for $800 to $1,000.

Felix Pets is a division of New York–based Transgenic Pets, which brought a lawsuit against Allerca over intellectual property issues in 2004. That suit was settled out of court for an undisclosed sum in 2005.

According to Young, Allerca had been pursuing genetic modification until [2005], when researchers ran into challenges silencing the allergen-producing gene. But it was during this research that Allerca developed genetic testing to focus on less potent versions of the Fel d 1 protein.

Contact with Pets

There are more than 100 million pets in the United States—that amounts to about four pets for every ten people.

Uncertain Effect on Cats

Little is known about the exact role the Fel d 1 protein plays in cats, so no one is sure what effect removing or suppressing the protein would have on an animal.

Duane Kraemer is a professor of veterinary physiology and pharmacology at Texas A&M University in College Station, and the owner of "CC," the world's first cloned cat.

"The only way to determine that would be to do some of the knockout experiments and see how the cats do," Kraemer said, referring to clinical trials in which a target protein is "knocked out" of an animal's genetic code.

UC Davis' Lyons agrees: "If [we learn] anything from these experiments these companies are doing, we might learn a lot about the physiology of this particular protein."

People with Allergies
Should Not Keep Cats

Carolyn Barry

Cats are known to be the leading source of pet allergies, but scientific research suggests that they are a bigger problem than previously suspected. In the following selection Carolyn Barry explains that a large-scale European study shows that cats make things worse for householders even if they do not feel symptoms of a cat allergy. The study found that people who were not directly allergic to cats nevertheless suffered poorer lung function if they had cats in their homes. No such result was found for other potential allergens, unless the occupants were actually allergic to them. More than eighteen hundred randomly selected volunteers and their homes were involved in the study, making it unlikely that the results are unrepresentative. Nevertheless, the scientists involved in the study say that its conclusions are only tentative and that more research is needed to confirm a cause-and-effect relationship between the presence of cats and poor lung function. Australian science writer Carolyn Barry earned a master's degree in journalism at the University of Colorado and went on to work in Washington, D.C., for the magazine *Science News*. She is now deputy editor of Australia's environmental monthly, *G Magazine*.

SOURCE: Carolyn Barry, "Cat Allergen Hits All Allergic People," *Science News*, July 7, 2007. Copyright © 2007 Science Service, Inc. Republished with permission of Science Service and the Public in the format Other Book via Copyright Clearance Center.

For people who have asthma or respiratory problems that are triggered by cats, living with Fluffy is obviously a bad idea. Now, researchers have found evidence suggesting that people who know that they have other allergies may also want to avoid the furry felines.

Scientists who conducted a study across 14 European countries say that people allergic to irritants such as dust mites, mold, and grass had poorer lung function if they were around cats than if they lived felinefree.

Surprising Results

"Cats are more of a problem than we thought," says lead author Sue Chinn of Imperial College London.

Recent research has shown that people living around cats performed worse on lung function tests even though they were not specifically allergic to cats. (© Ian West/ Alamy)

The unexpected result emerged from a broad study of allergy and lung function. The researchers went into the homes of 1,884 randomly selected volunteers and tested mattress-dust samples for allergens from cats and dust mites. Volunteers were also tested to determine whether they were allergic to common triggers such as dust mites, cats, Cladosporium mold, and timber grass, a relative of Kentucky bluegrass.

Scientists tested participants for allergies by measuring their blood concentrations of antibodies of a type known as immunoglobulin E (IgE). An allergic reaction occurs when an IgE antibody binds to an otherwise harmless compound and spurs the immune system into action.

Diminished Lung Function

To assess how living amid differing amounts of triggers affected participants' respiratory systems, the scientists had volunteers undergo a lung-function assessment that included a test of how strongly their lungs constricted in response to an irritant.

> **FAST FACT**
>
> A 2005 study found that exposure to cats prolongs the effects of asthma attacks for up to twenty-two hours.

Surprisingly, Chinn says, people living around cats performed worse on the lung function test even if they weren't specifically allergic to cats. By contrast, exposure to dust mites made no difference to the test results of people not allergic to the bugs.

The scientists had expected that people's lungs would constrict only when exposed to the stimulants that trigger their allergies, as happens in people with asthma.

More Studies Needed

Chinn cautions not to give away Fluffy just yet because "the study needs to be replicated before we start getting too excited." The results appear in the July [2007] *American Journal of Respiratory and Critical Care Medicine.*

Cat Allergies and Asthma

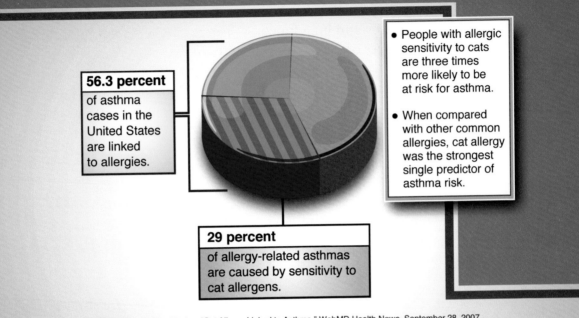

56.3 percent of asthma cases in the United States are linked to allergies.

29 percent of allergy-related asthmas are caused by sensitivity to cat allergens.

- People with allergic sensitivity to cats are three times more likely to be at risk for asthma.

- When compared with other common allergies, cat allergy was the strongest single predictor of asthma risk.

Taken from: Salynn Boyles, "Cat Allergy Linked to Asthma," WebMD Health News, September 28, 2007. www.webmd.com/asthma/news/20070928/cat-allergy-linked-to-asthma. (Data: National Health and Nutrition Examination Survey, 2005–2006.)

Dennis Ownby, a physician at the Medical College of Georgia in Augusta, notes that one of the more interesting findings of the study is that exposure to cats affected participants' breathing more than exposure to house dust mites did.

"For many years, a tremendous amount of work was done on mites in homes and the risk of asthma on the people living there," he says. "This study now suggests that mites are not that important."

The results don't necessarily indicate a cause-and-effect relationship, Ownby says. "It's possible that higher [sensitivities to] cat allergens are directly related to something else in the home and [that] we're just not measuring the primary culprit."

A Diet Based on Blood Type Can Fight Allergies

Peter J. D'Adamo

In the following selection naturopath Peter J. D'Adamo argues that blood type plays a significant role in the kind of allergy a person may be susceptible to. Blood types are distinguished by the presence or absence of various antigenic substances on the surface of red blood cells. Blood types are inherited and represent contributions from both parents. D'Adamo says that genetic factors are also influential over the development of food allergies and that blood type comes into play in determining which allergens are likeliest to flare into allergies. He also makes specific claims about other allergies, such as that people with blood type B are more susceptible to hay fever than others. By following a diet tailor-made for each blood type, he asserts, people can minimize their exposure. Peter J. D'Adamo is a naturopathic physician—that is, an alternative practitioner whose tradition calls for an emphasis on dietary cures.

SOURCE: Peter J. D'Adamo, *Allergies: Fight Them with the Blood Type Diet.* New York: G.P. Putnam's Sons, 2005. Copyright © 2005 by Hoop-A-Joop, LLC. Used by permission of Penguin Group (USA) Inc.

Your immune system can be likened to a modern army, composed of many different divisions that operate under the direction of a central command. Like the military, the immune system requires good intelligence. It must identify and attack the enemy, while at the same time preventing casualties from "friendly fire."

In a properly functioning immune system, B- and T-lymphocyte cells are responsible for detecting invaders and producing antibodies against them. When B-cells encounter something they perceive as foreign to the body —such as a bacteria, virus, etc.—they become plasma cells and secrete large quantities of antibodies. The antibodies are specific to the antigen and neutralize the foreign agent or destroy it. T-helper cells are involved in this response. TH-1 helper cells enhance the ability of the immune system to respond to infections or injury. TH-2 helper cells increase antibody production by releasing growth factors that increase antibody production. When these T-helper cells become overactive, they produce the immune system equivalent of friendly fire. No longer able to distinguish between friend or foe, they destroy the cells of "self."

The allergic reaction is related to this hyperactive response. The immune system of an allergic person reacts defensively when a particular allergen is present, producing large quantities of a special class of antibodies called immunoglobulin E (IgE). Different IgE antibodies are produced for each type of allergen, whether it's latex, pet dander, oak pollen, or ragweed pollen. IgE molecules are specific for the original allergen and can readily bind to the allergen that caused their production.

Repeat Performance

These allergen-specific IgE molecules travel through the blood and attach to receptors on the surface of mast cells—cells found in most body tissues, which synthesize and release histamine, a chemical that produces the classic symptoms of watery eyes, sneezing, welts, and hives. Once allergen-specific IgE has attached to the mast cell surface, it can remain for weeks or even months, always ready to bind to the original allergen. The next time the original allergen enters the body, the allergic cascade begins, and again results in the release of histamines from the mast cell. The symptoms may occur in just minutes, or up to an hour after contact. . . .

Food Allergies

The genetic predisposition to food allergies is well documented. In households where both parents are allergic, 67 percent of the offspring are allergic. Where one parent is allergic, 33 percent of the offspring are allergic. Immunologically produced food reactions result from the reaction of the food substance with sensitized IgE antibodies located on circulating mast cells. This leads to immediate hypersensitivity, so called because most of the symptoms develop within thirty to ninety minutes of ingesting the offending food. These symptoms include the well-known anaphylaxis symptoms of allergy—bronchial congestion and asthma, hives and eczema, headaches, loss of memory, and spaciness. (These reactions are caused by immune reactions, as opposed to other causes, such as inadequate stomach acid or esophageal reflux.)

Other conditions commonly associated with food allergies include such diverse problems as low back pain, bed-wetting, chronic bladder infections, canker sores, middle ear infections, asthma, acne, headache, and duodenal ulcers. Some of the common physical signs of allergy are dark circles or puffiness under the eyes, horizontal creases in the lower eyelid, swollen glands, and fluid retention.

However, the majority of so-called allergies are actually intolerances. Often, patients will come to my clinic complaining of allergies when technically they have intolerances or hypersensitivities. What is the difference?

Simply put, a true allergy involves the activation of the IgE antibodies, whereas an intolerance does not. However, this doesn't mean that an intolerance is less serious or that it doesn't involve an immune reaction. For example, the problem some people have digesting the lactose in milk is not due to a lactose *allergy*. Rather, these individuals lack the specific enzyme needed to break it down. They are lactose *intolerant*.

Lectins in the Blood

Most people have more to fear from hidden lectins entering their systems than from food allergies. Lectins are proteins in many foods that can bind to sugars (including blood type antigens) and cause cell damage.

According to the *British Journal of Nutrition*, which published a recent review of the subject, evidence exists that dietary lectins play a significant role in autoimmune and inflammatory diseases. The study seemed to indicate that interaction between dietary lectins and the cells lining the intestines may unnecessarily "rev up" the immune system and activate autoantibodies. Several dietary lectins, including those in peas and peanuts, have been shown to increase immunoglobulin A (IgA). IgA is the antibody most involved in the health of the digestive system. It is the main antibody in a variety of secretions such as saliva, milk, and the mucus lining the airways and digestive tract. Two common components of wheat, gliandin and gluten, have also been shown in repeated studies to increase the production of IgA.

Dietary lectins have also been shown to induce the production of interleukin-4, which in turn activates IgE. This may explain why one of the more common benefits reported by those who follow the Blood Type Diet is a lessening of allergic manifestations, sinusitis, and asthma. Many bacteria use lectins to attach to host tissue, and these lectins are some of the more highly allergenic parts of the organism. Many food lectins trigger IgE, including the lectins found in bananas, chestnuts, and avocados. They are all implicated in what has been termed "latex fruit allergies." Kiwi fruit lectins can also trigger IgE.

Lectins from peas, broad beans, lentils, jack beans, soy beans, peanuts, and wheat germ have been shown to bind directly with IgE and initiate the release of histamine, which can produce a feeling of spaciness, a condition characterized by an inability to focus and concentrate.

One of the most damaging effects of dietary lectins is a condition known as leaky gut syndrome. This occurs when partially digested proteins cross the intestinal barrier and are absorbed into the bloodstream. The mucus lining of the intestine consists of helpful bacteria and good yeasts that break down the food into substances that are used beneficially by the body's systems. When the composition of this lining is disturbed, the intestinal walls can be damaged and become porous. Overwhelmed

Lectins from peas and beans bind directly with immunoglobulin E and initiate the release of histamines, which can cause an inability to focus or concentrate.
(© BrandX/SuperStock)

by the flood of foreign substances, the immune system overreacts, causing allergic reactions at the site of transfer, at distant sites, or systemically. . . .

Role of Blood Type

Nature has endowed our immune systems with very sophisticated methods to determine if a substance in the body is foreign or not. One method involves looking for chemical markers called antigens, which are found on the cells of our bodies and on most other living things. Any substance could be an antigen; the only requirement is that it be unique enough to allow the immune system an opportunity to determine if it is "self" or "non-self."

All life forms, from the simplest virus to humans, have unique antigens that form a part of their chemical fingerprint. Among the many antigens in your body is one that determines blood type. When your immune system is attempting to identify a suspicious character, one of the first things it looks for is your blood type antigen.

> **FAST FACT**
>
> Blood types were discovered by Austrian scientist Karl Landsteiner in 1901. His discovery paved the way for safe blood transfusions.

Each blood type is determined by the presence or absence of an antigen with a unique chemical structure composed of long chains of a repeating sugar called fucose, which by itself forms the O antigen of Blood Type O. Fucose also serves as the base for the other blood types. Blood Type A is composed of fucose, plus a sugar named N-acetyl galactosamine. Blood Type B is fucose, plus a different sugar named D-galactosamine. Blood Type AB is fucose, plus N-acetyl galactosamine, plus D-galactosamine.

Each blood type antigen creates opposing antibodies to other blood type antigens. These anti–blood type antibodies are often called isohemagglutinins because they are made throughout life and are IgM antibodies, so they can agglutinate antigens directly. These are very powerful antibodies!

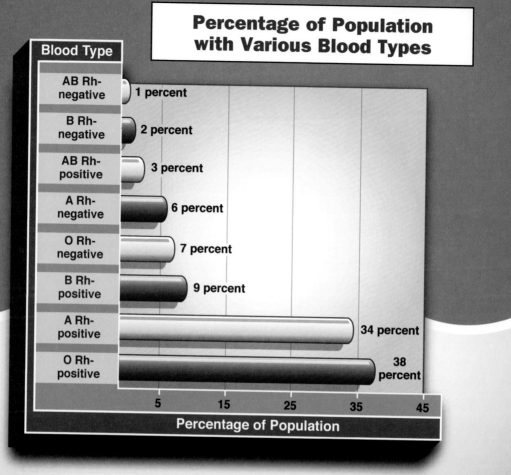

Percentage of Population with Various Blood Types

Blood Type	Percentage of Population
AB Rh-negative	1 percent
B Rh-negative	2 percent
AB Rh-positive	3 percent
A Rh-negative	6 percent
O Rh-negative	7 percent
B Rh-positive	9 percent
A Rh-positive	34 percent
O Rh-positive	38 percent

Taken from: Bloodcenters.org, "Percentage by Blood Type," April 27, 2007. www.swivel.com.

The best known role of the isohemagglutinins is seen in the transfusion reaction. This occurs when someone is inadvertently given the wrong blood type during a transfusion. This process can be very serious. A person who receives an incompatible blood transfusion may experience fever, shaking, chills, shortness of breath, hives, and nausea. Shock, kidney failure, or blood coagulation can ensue, and even death may occur, although rare. . . .

Blood Type and Lectins

While some lectins react with the tissues of all blood types, many lectins are blood type–specific, in that they show a clear preference for one kind of sugar over another and mechanically fit the antigen of one blood type or another. This blood type specificity results in their attaching to the antigen of a preferred blood type, while leaving other blood type antigens completely undisturbed. At the cellular level, a common effect of lectins is to provoke the sugars on the surface of one cell to cross-link with those of another, effectively causing the cells to stick together and agglutinate. Not all lectins cause agglutination; many bacteria have lectinlike receptors that they use to attach to the cells of their host. Other lectins, called mitogens, cause a proliferation of certain cells of the immune system. But, in the most basic sense, lectins make things stick to other things. . . .

Blood Type O

Blood Type O is more prone to inflammation than the other blood types and tends to have higher levels of IgE and IgA. This vulnerability is possibly related to the fucose sugar that acts as its blood type antigen. Fucose sugars are known to serve as adhesion molecules for selectins, [a certain type of lectin] allowing the hyperactive migration of white blood cells from the bloodstream into areas of infection, which in turn causes inflammation. Studies have shown that Blood Type O individuals tend to dramatically increase the levels of their anti-A and anti-B antibodies during infections.

Blood Type O individuals are more likely to be asthma sufferers, and even hay fever, the bane of so many, appears to be specific to Type O blood. A wide range of pollens contains lectins that stimulate the release of the powerful histamines that lead to the common allergy symptoms. Many food lectins, especially wheat, interact with IgE antibodies found in Type O blood. These antibodies stimulate white blood cells called basophiles to release not only histamines but also other powerful chemical allergens called kinins. These can cause severe allergic reactions, swelling the tissues of the throat and constricting the lungs. Type Os who eliminate wheat from their diets often relieve many of their allergy symptoms, such as sneezing, respiratory problems, snoring, or persistent digestive disorders.

Digestively, Blood Type O's extreme sensitivity to the lectins in wheat and corn makes them more vulnerable to inflammatory conditions such as leaky gut syndrome and increases their susceptibility to irritable bowel syndrome and Crohn's disease.

According to research, non-secretor [lacking blood type antigens in nonblood body fluids] status plays a prominent role in Blood Type O's susceptibility to allergies.

Blood Type A

There are several pathways to allergies for Blood Type A. One is the tendency to produce high levels of selectins in response to infection or injury. Overproduction of selectins, E-selectin in particular, produces a hyperactive or inflammatory response. Several components of the diet are known to influence selectin levels. High animal protein diets further increase E-selectin, while a diet featuring more soy protein significantly lowers selectin levels. One important component of soy, the isoflavone genestein, inhibits enzymes necessary to increase selectins and other vascular adhesion molecules.

Blood Type A children (or even children with Blood Type A mothers) are more prone to develop ear infections. In general, Blood Type A children have about a 50 percent higher rate of infection. Strains of bacteria most likely to cause ear infections have a very strong preference for the Blood Type A antigen. This is especially true for non-secretors. A contributory trigger is Blood Type A's tendency to produce copious amounts of mucus, which can exacerbate ear infections and certain respiratory conditions. In Blood Type A children, dairy products are often the culprit in excessive mucus production.

Blood Type A also has a predisposition to bronchial asthma in childhood, and Type A individuals are generally more asthmatic.

Digestively, Blood Type A individuals who consume too much animal protein—especially red meat—tend to suffer from leaky gut syndrome. Type As have low levels of digestive enzymes, making it difficult for them to digest meat. The result is undigested proteins that take far too long to transit the intestines and eliminate from the system.

Blood Type B

Overall, Blood Type B is associated with greater severity of chronic inflammatory diseases of the lungs, including bronchial asthma and pollinosis. Research shows that Blood Type B has a higher susceptibility to grass pollen hay fever than do the other blood types. Often the trigger is dietary, as Blood Type B individuals have intense sensitivities to a diverse number of lectins, such as those found in chicken, corn, wheat, soy, and peanuts.

Blood Type B's susceptibility to viral infection appears to be related to their sensitivity to a class of agglutinins called galectins, found in all animals but most notably found in chicken meat. Galectins are considered a type of "internal lectin" made by higher animals and used for a variety of specialized functions, especially within the liver. They bind several different galactose-antigens, and it is probably for this reason that chicken seems to agglutinate the cells of Blood Types B and AB. Several galectins are known to involve themselves in the inflammatory process. For example, urinary tract infections, to which Blood Type B individuals are prone, are known triggers for subsequent inflammatory diseases.

Blood Type AB

Blood Type AB has the highest resistance to respiratory allergies of all the blood types. However, Blood Type AB is somewhat susceptible to the conditions related to both the A and B antigens. Like Blood Type A, Type AB has a tendency toward overstimulation of selectins on the blood vessel walls, which allows excessive white blood cell migration into the tissues and triggers inflammation. Blood Type AB also shares the Type A tendency for overproduction of mucus and somewhat lower than normal levels of stomach acid. Like Blood Type B, Type AB is susceptible to viral and bacterial infections, and these in turn can trigger autoimmune inflammatory responses, often through inactivating complement or blocking the liver's ability to detoxify normal metabolic waste products.

More than the other blood types, Blood Type AB is affected by diminished activity of natural killer (NK) cells. NK cells are a subset of T-lymphocytes, which function as a first line of defense against infection. . . .

The ultimate goal of any treatment must go beyond just getting over the latest bout with illness. That's where the Blood Type Diet comes in. If you are being treated for allergies, sinusitis, asthma, or related conditions, talk to your physician about incorporating these long-term strategies into your program.

The Blood Type Diet and its related lifestyle/supplement strategies can help you fight allergies by:

Attacking the underlying causes of allergies The Blood Type Diet promotes a healthy immune system, reducing the potential for infections that can trigger the inflammatory process.

Relieving allergy symptoms Adhering to the diet that is right for your blood type is a proven way to relieve symptoms by eliminating immunoreactive lectins that trigger allergic responses.

Alleviating the need for allergy medications Antihistamines, antacids, antibiotics, corticosteroids, and other medications can have damaging side effects. Frequently, those who follow the Blood Type Diet experience major relief of symptoms and no longer need these medications.

(A caveat: Never discontinue prescription medications without consulting your physician.)

Establishing overall health and fitness The Blood Type Diet utilizes the best of naturopathic medicine, combined with individualized diet, exercise, and lifestyle strategies that support maximum health. The Blood Type Diet is nutritionally tailored to emphasize foods that support digestive, immune, and metabolic balance.

A Diet Based on Blood Type Cannot Fight Allergies

Michael Klaper

In the following selection, physician Michael Klaper attacks the idea that a diet based on blood type can have any therapeutic value for treating allergies or other maladies. The claim that people of different blood types represent different dietary ancestries is overbroad, he argues. Moreover, there is no scientific evidence to support the claim that blood type is implicated in the frequency of food allergies or other diet-related difficulties, he states. After graduating from the University of Illinois College of Medicine in Chicago in 1972, Michael Klaper became increasingly concerned about the role of the standard American diet in disease. He has since become an advocate of low-fat vegetarian therapies.

The "blood type diet" theory has gained widespread attention from the public since the release of "Eat Right For Your Type" by Peter J. D'Adamo, N. D. (G. P. Putnam's Sons, New York, 1996). The book's basic premise—that Type O's are the dominant, hunter-caveman type that requires meat in the diet, Type A's are docile vegetarians, and Type B's are dairy-eating omnivores —has become a dietary manifesto for many people. However, the "blood type diet" theory, and the book that promotes it, presents many problems that prevent me from seriously basing any of my dietary choices upon them.

Author D'Adamo hangs much of his theory on the action of lectins, which are sugar-containing proteins found on the surface of certain foods that can cause various molecules and some types of cells to stick together. He blames lectins for serious disruptions throughout the body, from agglutination of the blood cells to cirrhosis and kidney failure. . . . D'Adamo states that, ". . . certain beans and legumes, especially lentils and kidney beans, contain lectins that deposit in your muscle tissues, making them more alkaline and less charged for physical activity." This is quite a serious scientific charge, and an alarming thought if you are blood Type O—namely, that after eating a bowl of bean chili or lentil stew, lectin proteins are depositing in your muscles and altering their function, changing their acidity, and diminishing your capability for physical action.

Lack of Evidence

If one is going to make a statement like that—and publish it in a book destined for the bestseller list, with the intent of changing the eating habits of a nation—I believe the author is obliged to present solid scientific evidence that supports that assertion. . . . A statement that potentially will frighten millions of Type O readers about eating kidney beans, lentils, and wheat should be supported by photographs taken through a powerful (electron) microscope. These photomicrographs would show muscle tissue biopsied from people with Type O, Type A, Type B, and Type AB blood after they have eaten kidney beans and/or lentils. (Sampling of muscle fibers, fat tissue,

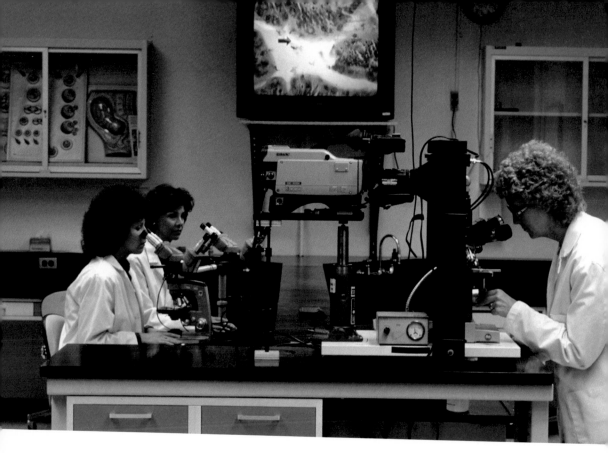

To prove that lectins found on certain legumes and beans negatively affect the muscle function of Type O individuals, scientists will need to thoroughly research the issue and conduct studies. (© Phototake, Inc./Alamy)

etc., is a common, safe, and virtually painless technique, known as "skinny needle" biopsy, and is routinely performed on paid volunteers by researchers in nutrition, exercise physiology, pharmacology, aging, and other sciences.) The photographs would clearly show the lectin deposits in the muscles of people with Type O blood—and little or no deposits in the tissue samples from the muscles of people with Type A blood. If an author cannot produce proof like this, or clearly cite the scientific references in the text where other people have demonstrated such proof, his credibility, to me, is severely diminished. D'Adamo presents neither photos nor corroborating studies to support his speculations.

Research Not There

To substantiate the assertion that lectins change the muscles, "making them more alkaline and less charged for physical activity," the author would need to publish his own research or cite other scientific studies wherein tiny microelectrodes that measure acidity inside the cells were inserted into the muscles of paid human volunteers of various blood types. All subjects would be fed a meal of lentils and kidney beans, and a significantly greater shift towards alkalinity would be observed in the muscles of the Type O subjects. Yet, no such studies are cited or presented.

Misplaced Fears

If an author doesn't have this kind of proof, is it responsible for him to make statements that may frighten millions of people away from eating high-protein, high-fibre legumes and other potentially valuable foods? Indeed, it may be best for a particular person not to eat a particular legume—but the reason he or she should refrain from doing so should be for solid nutritional/medical reasons —like true allergies, colitis, etc. and not because of their ABO blood type.

D'Adamo's book contains many scientifically unsatisfying, "one size fits all" statements, like that on page 63, "Type O's do not tolerate whole wheat products at all." Such a statement prompts the question, "What does he mean, 'at all?'" Do Type O's eat a whole wheat cracker and fall on the ground holding their abdomen and vomiting —or worse yet, suffer immediate brain damage due to their blood cells agglutinating throughout their brain? How much wheat can a Type O eat before their blood agglutinates? One hamburger bun? One noodle?

True Allergy May Be Cause

I'm not denying that many people do experience digestive or other problems when they eat wheat. They do indeed, but the reason is because they have a true wheat allergy, gluten intolerance, or some other verifiable mechanism —not because of some sugar and protein molecules sticking up from the surface of their red blood cells. Like

D'Adamo, I grant that wheat can be a problematic food for people with colitis, and I often recommend eliminating it from the diet. Lectins may even play a role in the inflammatory process for some people. However, before one tells millions of individuals with Type O blood to never eat whole wheat—many of whom apparently have no difficulty with whole wheat and who rely on breads as a major source of energy and protein—isn't some convincing scientific proof required? I feel that author D'Adamo at least owes his readers a text citation with supporting evidence that wheat-induced colon dysfunction is a condition peculiar to Type O's. Yet, his text is devoid of scientific endnote citations. . . .

Blood Clot Plot

What finally pushes the "blood type" theory beyond the limits of believability for me is the primary mechanism of physiologic damage that D'Adamo postulates—namely, lectin proteins on some foods causing blood agglutination in certain people of blood types who are "not genetically/evolutionarily suited" to eat those foods. This is a very serious—and potentially life-threatening —phenomenon that the author proposes. Agglutination means that the red cells in your bloodstream are irreversibly sticking together and forming clumps. Once they begin to clump together, they don't come apart. (Note that this is very different than blood sludging, or so-called rouleoux formation—a phenomenon seen when the surface of the red cells become coated with fat or other substances to make them sticky enough to temporarily and reversibly adhere to each other's surfaces—but not to become permanently bonded through irreversible intertwining of surface proteins, which is what happens in agglutination.)

Having your blood agglutinate as it circulates through your body is not conducive to good health—or, for that matter, to long-term survival. What is so bad about little

Distribution of Blood Types by Rh (Plus or Minus)

Blood Type	Rh Type	Percentage
A	+	34
A	−	6
B	+	9
B	−	2
AB	+	3
AB	−	1
O	+	38
O	−	7

Taken from: NASA, "Graphic Blood and Its Type," accessed May 5, 2008. http://nasaexplorers.com/show_58_teacher_st.php?id=04901124418.

clumps of red blood cells sailing through the bloodstream? Red blood cells deliver oxygen to the cells of vital tissues like the brain, heart and kidneys. To accomplish this delivery, they must flow through the tiniest of blood vessels—microscopic capillaries so narrow that the red blood cells must line up single file to get through. If the red blood cells are being agglutinated by lectins (or anything else), clumps of red cells will clog up the capillaries and block the blood flow. Thus, the blood stream will be prevented from delivering its life-sustaining cargo of oxygen and nutrients to the tissues served by those obstructed capillaries. Cells deprived of oxygen become damaged, and soon die. (Cell death is called "infarction" of tissue.)

Since most people are unaware of their blood types (let alone what foods are "evolutionarily inappropriate" for them to eat), it is reasonable to assume that on most days most people eat the "wrong foods" for their blood type (e.g., Type O's eating wheat, Type A's eating meat, etc.). Thus, according to D'Adamo's theory, most everyone experiences repeated showers of agglutinated red cells throughout their bloodstream after most every meal—day after day, month after month, year after year. If the vital capillary beds in your heart, lungs, kidneys, brain, eyes, and other essential organs are subjected to barrage after barrage of agglutinated red blood cells, they will eventually begin to clog up. These micro-areas of diminished blood flow would at first cause scattered, then more concentrated areas of tissue damage and destruction—with eventually many micro-infarctions scattered throughout these vital structures. Over time, the brain, heart, lungs, kidneys and adrenals would be irreparably scarred and fibrosed by these processes—resulting in multi-organ failure and potentially fatal outcomes in millions of people. . . .

> **FAST FACT**
>
> In addition to the four major blood types, scientists have identified at least 276 discrete red-cell antigens, leading one skeptic of the blood type diet to wonder if we need 276 discrete diets for our health.

An Incredible Tale

In my opinion, D'Adamo has spun an evolutionary fairy tale that leaves many unanswered questions. What exactly is he proposing happened to Type O hunter-gatherers when the Type A people began growing wheat, barley and other grains? Do Type O people eat a mouthful of barley and fall down in the dust, unable to work and reproduce? Do they then become warlike and club the agrarian people to death because lectins are clogging their intestines? Do the genetic changes to Type A blood type magically appear just before a society grows new grains (allowing them to eat the new grains in the first place), or did Type A blood types emerge after the grains are grown, as the people with Type O blood died out from their blood agglutinating in their brains? And why would so many of the native Indians of North America, classic Type O hunters, go to the trouble of cultivating high-lectin corn (maize)?

If you find all the foregoing questions as troubling as I do, perhaps you, too, will want to think long and hard about adopting the "blood type" diet as your guide for health-enhancing dietary choices.

Food Allergies Are Authentic

DukeHealth.org

In the next selection the Duke University Health Center's online news service describes the extent of the food allergy threat. For an allergic child the threat can be life-threatening unless emergency medical treatment is administered. An estimated 11 million Americans suffer from food allergies, the selection states. Food allergies start as early as six months after birth and may continue for life—especially with certain foods, such as dairy products, eggs, and peanut butter. Some children outgrow their allergies, but for many others the malady requires lifelong management. So far, a cure has not been found. Dukehealth.org, a service of the Duke University Health Center, is managed by Duke Creative, an agency serving the university.

When Eric Nguyen was a toddler, just one bite of a piece of chocolate with nuts triggered a medical emergency.

SOURCE: "Foiling Food Allergies," DukeHealth.org, March 8, 2006. Copyright © 2004–2008 Duke University Health System. Reproduced by permission.

His mother, Theresa, recalls, "Within maybe 15 minutes, he was itching like crazy, with hives from top to bottom." Gasping for breath, Eric was rushed to the emergency room for a lifesaving shot of epinephrine.

For Eric's little brother, mere cooking vapors did it.

"My husband was cooking shrimp, and I was folding the laundry, and Conrad was just running around, laughing and giggling, and I said to my husband, 'His voice is getting higher pitched,'" says Theresa. "The next thing I knew he was flat on the floor, passed out."

As it turned out, all three of Theresa Nguyen's children —Eric, now 17, Tessa, 15, and Conrad, 13—have allergies to such foods as peanuts, eggs, milk, and shellfish.

> **FAST FACT**
>
> According to the Asthma and Allergy Foundation of America, from 3 percent to 8 percent of children have reactions to some foods.

Millions Afflicted

Recognizing that those allergies can be life-threatening has motivated Nguyen to work closely with allergists, research causes and treatments for food allergies, learn to cook allergen-free foods, join support groups, and educate teachers and nurses in her children's schools about adjusting to children with such allergies.

A growing number of families are making these adjustments. Studies show that eleven million Americans have food allergies and one-and-a-half million have a peanut allergy. According to the Food Allergy and Anaphylaxis Network (FAAN), from 1997 to 2002 the incidence of peanut allergy in children had doubled.

Duke's Wesley Burks, MD, chief of pediatric allergy and immunology, says that food allergies typically appear between six and 18 months of age, since that is when many youngsters first sample foods such as peanut butter.

While children often outgrow certain food allergies, such as to eggs and milk, peanut allergies are usually for life.

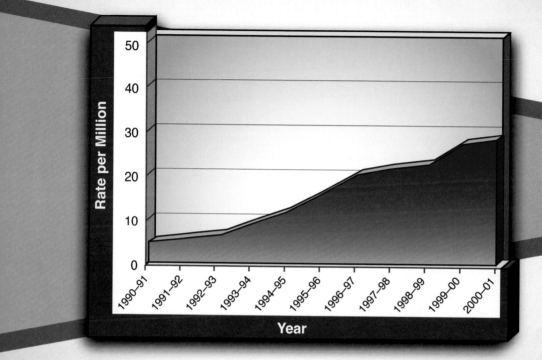

Hospital Admissions for Food Allergies on the Rise in Britain

Taken from: Ramyani Gupta, Aziz Sheikh, and David Strachan, "Increasing Hospital Admissions for Systemic Allergic Disorders in England: Analysis of National Admissions Data," *British Medical Journal*, 2003. http://bmj.bmjjournals.com/cgi/content/full/327/7424/1142.

Diagnosing the Allergy

Not every reaction to a food is an allergy. A detailed clinical history is needed to differentiate viral gastroenteritis or food poisoning from food allergies.

"You need to find out the timing of the ingestion and the clinical symptoms," Burks says. "Reactions to an allergen such as peanuts occur literally within minutes, not more than an hour or two, after ingestion. Food allergy symptoms are also isolated to the GI [gastrointestinal] tract, the respiratory tract, and the skin."

These symptoms include abdominal cramps, vomiting, diarrhea, skin symptoms like hives or itchy rash, difficulty breathing, and swelling of the lips or the eyes.

Also, "Food-allergy symptoms are reproducible," Burks says. "Each time they have the food, they ought to have fairly similar symptoms."

Taking a good clinical history means tuning in to the patient. "The thing I like as a parent is that Dr. Burks will talk with the kids himself," Nguyen says. "I'm sitting there, but his conversation is with the kids, asking them for their contribution in terms of what's bothering them or what they want help with."

Diagnosis also depends on tests to measure the blood level of the immune protein IgE that triggers allergic reactions, and skin tests for sensitivity.

A laboratory technician processes tissue samples as part of diagnostic testing for allergies. (© Olaf Doering/Alamy)

Nguyen's family focuses on lifestyle adjustments. Conrad cannot even be in the same room with peanuts, so he takes his school lunch outside with a friend. Eric always carries his medicine and his EpiPen [epinephrine self-injector]. And they all look out for each other; Tessa, for example, is learning to cook treats that her brothers can eat.

Changing attitudes is also critical—among physicians, school administrators, and managers of any public facilities, says Nguyen, who has dealt with a physician who, despite detailed medical records, dismissed the idea that Conrad had a severe peanut allergy.

"Food allergies are real, and people with them should be treated no differently than somebody with diabetes or heart disease," she says. "It's a medical condition that we deal with as part of our life."

In Search of Treatments

While Nguyen fights false perceptions, Burks develops future treatments, including a vaccine.

After identifying the predominant allergy-triggering proteins in peanuts, Burks and collaborators are experimenting with altering the protein so that it will dampen the response of immune system cells, to avoid tripping the allergic alarm.

These experiments could lead to a vaccine in which the altered peanut protein could be given to allergy sufferers to desensitize them to peanuts.

More immediately, the researchers are clinically testing a therapy in which patients ingest tiny amounts of egg or peanut protein orally in an attempt to gradually desensitize their immune systems.

So far, patients have had minimal symptoms, Burks says. While initial protein doses are the equivalent of about a hundredth of a peanut, after three months, patients can consume an entire peanut each day as part of the treatment.

"We know we're changing their immune systems in some way over those three months," says Burks, "but only longer-term studies will tell us whether the tolerance is permanent."

Burks cautions that there will be no magic bullet against food allergies. Immunotherapies, drug therapies, vigilance against allergens, and preparation for allergic attacks will always be part of the arsenal.

Still, says Burks, "I think that in five years we'll have combinations of treatments that will prove effective."

Food Allergies Are Exaggerated

Meredith Broussard

Parents have the impression that food allergy is an epidemic that threatens their children's lives. In the selection that follows, Meredith Broussard dismisses those fears as unwarranted. Noting that only about a dozen children a year die of food allergy complications, she argues that the fear of allergies has been pumped up. Part of the problem is that the public often confuses food allergy with food intolerance. There is a significant difference between the two, Broussard says. More serious, however, is what Broussard says is an advocacy campaign through the news media to stir up an unwarranted fear of a food allergy epidemic. Meredith Broussard is a Philadelphia-based journalist and writer.

O f little concern to most parents or educators only a generation ago, food allergies are now seen as a childhood epidemic. The American Academy of

Pediatrics recently began recommending that peanuts be withheld until a child turns three; hundreds of food-allergy nonprofits and local parents groups have formed; and six states have passed laws requiring food-allergy safety measures in their schools, with similar legislation currently being considered in Congress. Children are even being recruited to help battle this supposed threat, as in this Food Allergy & Anaphylaxis Network (FAAN) brochure, which enjoins young students to "Be a PAL" and protect the lives of their classmates. But the rash of fatal food allergies is mostly myth, a cultural hysteria cooked up with a few key ingredients: fearful parents in an age of increased anxiety, sensationalist news coverage, and a coterie of well-placed advocates whose dubious science has fed the frenzy.

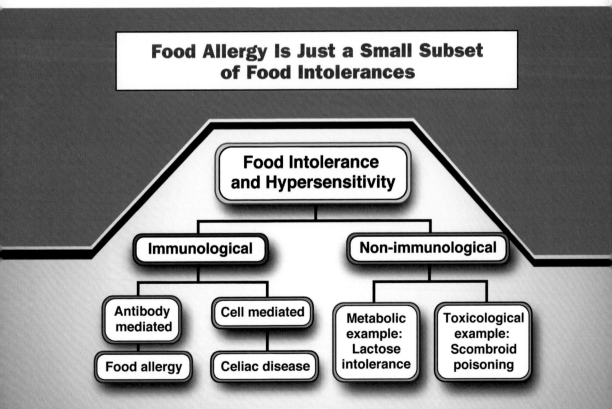

Food Allergy Is Just a Small Subset of Food Intolerances

Taken from: Threshold Working Group, "Approaches to Establish Thresholds for Major Food Allergens and for Gluten in Food," U.S. Food and Drug Administration, June 2005. www.cfsan.fda.gov/~dms/alrgn.html.

Media Impact

One of the first and most influential of the food-allergy nonprofits, FAAN has successfully passed off as fact its message that food allergies have become more prevalent and dire. Since 2005, more than 400 news stories have used FAAN's estimates that allergic reactions to food send 30,000 Americans to emergency rooms each year and that 150 to 200 ultimately die. The group derived these figures from a 1999 study of a rural Minnesota community, in which 133 people over a five-year period were determined to have suffered anaphylaxis—an allergic reaction that can mean everything from going into shock to developing an itchy mouth. Yet only nine people in the study ever required hospitalization for anaphylaxis from any cause. As for the death estimate, just one person died of anaphylactic shock, prompted not by food allergies but by exercise. The Centers for Disease Control and Prevention [CDC], in its most up-to-date figures, recorded only 12 deaths from food allergies in all of 2004. When asked about these statistical discrepancies, FAAN founder and CEO [chief executive officer] Anne Muñoz-Furlong said focusing on any number misses the point: "One child dying from food allergies is too many."

Popular Myth

In 2005, every major American media outlet covered the story of a teenager who died after kissing a boy who earlier in the day had eaten a peanut-butter sandwich. This "kiss of death" confirmed for countless nervous parents their worst fears: food-allergic children were in constant danger—they could "even die!" as FAAN warns here—from any sort of secondhand exposure to certain foods. (In a press release soon after the girl's death, FAAN instructed food-allergic teens to tell "that special someone that you can die. . . . Don't wait for the first kiss.") But there is simply no evidence that a food allergen can do serious harm if not ingested. Nicholas Pawlowski, an allergist at Children's Hospital of Philadelphia, says he occasionally has to spread peanut butter on a patient's arm to demonstrate to parents that their child will not die from casual contact with a nut. In the case of the peanut-butter kiss, a coroner later ruled, to no fanfare, that the girl had smoked pot soon before the embrace and actually died from an asthma attack.

In addition to offering certificates to "PAL Heroes," FAAN presents individuals and businesses with a service award named after Muñoz-Furlong's daughter, a former food-allergic child who, like most people, grew out of her allergies. Anne Muñoz-Furlong says she founded FAAN when her community didn't seem to believe that the threat to her child was real. Her organization and others have certainly helped to change the perception of food allergies. (A recent *Newsweek* cover showing a pigtailed girl in a gas mask with a carton of milk in one hand and a peanut-butter sandwich in the other is typical of much recent coverage.) But all we know for certain now is that more parents *think* their children suffer from food allergies. Indeed, even the best allergy tests produce high rates of false positives, and most studies of childhood prevalence interview no one under the age of eighteen. Ken Kochanek, a CDC statistician, says there are far too few recorded incidents of anaphylactic shock triggered by food allergies to draw any sound epidemiological conclusions: "We can't find any hard data that supports the severity.". . .

Industry Funding

The FAAN children's website was built using a donation from Dey, the distributor of the EpiPen adrenaline injector; Dey and Verus Pharmaceuticals, the maker of EpiPen's chief competitor, sponsor FAAN's major annual fundraising event. (As part of its safety guidelines, FAAN suggests carrying an adrenaline injector at all times and regularly renewing the prescription.) Just about all

An allergy sufferer uses the EpiPen self-injector after an anaphylactic allergic reaction. (© Papa Kay/Alamy)

the leading food allergists also have ties to FAAN or the Food Allergy Initiative (FAI), an organization prone to even more extreme rhetoric. This intimacy helps explain why suspect statistical findings get published. For instance, the coauthors of an oft-cited study on the dangers facing food-allergic children at restaurants were Anne Muñoz-Furlong's husband, who serves as a top FAAN executive, and a FAAN medical-board member whose research is funded in part by FAI. The latter is also an editor at the leading allergy journal where the study appeared; the journal's editor-in-chief is head of FAI's medical board.

Harmful Exaggeration

There is no question that food allergies are real. Yet instead of creating healthy, happy children . . . exaggerating the threat may actually do as much harm as the allergies themselves. The peril is now perceived as so great that psychosomatic reactions to foods and their odors are not uncommon. Recent surveys have also shown that children thought to have food allergies feel more overwhelmed by anxiety, more limited in what they believe they can safely accomplish, than even children with diabetes and rheumatological disease. One study documented how food-allergic youths become terror-stricken when inside places like supermarkets and restaurants, since they know that allergens are nearby. Such psychological distress is exacerbated by parents, who report keeping their children away from birthday parties and sending them to school in "No Nuts" T-shirts. Having been fed a steady diet of fear for more than two decades, we have become, it appears, what we eat.

> **FAST FACT**
>
> Food-borne illnesses are a far more deadly threat than food allergies. Bacteria such as salmonella are responsible for approximately five thousand deaths in the United States each year.

Overcleaning Homes May Lead to More Allergies

Mary Bufe

Allergies are triggered by allergens in our surrounding environment. So one might think that keeping the home environment pristine would prevent allergies. In the following selection, however, Mary Bufe presents the case that the opposite is true. According to scientists that she quotes, too much cleanliness deprives children of the opportunity to get sick and thereby develop their immune systems to the point that they can resist overreacting to various potential allergens. When they later encounter them an allergy develops. This "hygiene hypothesis" has not won universal acceptance, she notes, but there is evidence to support it. Writer Mary Bufe is a regular contributor to *Water Environment & Technology*.

Mom would be so proud. All her nagging about washing our hands and cleaning behind our ears seems to have finally sunk in—perhaps too much.

SOURCE: Mary Bufe, "Sick from Being Too Clean?" *Water Environment & Technology*, Fall 2005. Copyright © 2008 WEF. Reproduced by permission.

In fact, some scientists now believe that many of us are too clean, coating every household surface with anti-bacterial cleansers to stop the spread of germs and limiting our children's contact with daycare centers, farm animals, and the great outdoors. And that's a problem, these scientists say. According to their "hygiene hypothesis," the cleaner, more sanitary environments we now live in have greatly minimized children's exposure to dirt, bacteria, and other infection-causing agents that may actually benefit their developing immune systems.

FAST FACT

Household cleaning agents may help rid the home of organic allergens, but the agents themselves can cause allergic reactions in some people.

The repeated exposure to microbes at an early age, they theorize, actually helps children's immune systems develop properly. Without it, their immune systems can be over-stimulated by harmless substances like pollen and other environmental stimuli, resulting in the development of allergies and asthma. At least, that's the theory.

Allergies on the Rise

There's no question that allergies and asthma are on the rise in this country and elsewhere. The Centers for Disease Control and Prevention (Atlanta) has reported that the prevalence of asthma in the United States more than doubled over a recent 20-year period, from about 6.8 million cases in 1978 to more than 15 million in 1998. About 5% of the U.S. population now have the condition, the highest percentage of which are children between the ages of 5 and 14. But can this increase be attributed to overzealous hygiene?

Dwight D. Bowman, professor of parasitology at the Cornell University College of Veterinary Medicine (Ithaca, N.Y.) is one scientist who tends to think so. He longs for the days when children built strong immune systems, in part, by getting dirty. "Years ago, most of our veterinary students came from farms," he noted. "They grew up around cows and other farm animals. So being around these animals at school had no impact on them."

Today, however, Bowman says it is a different story. Most of his students' first hands-on exposure to farm animals is when they arrive at veterinary school. "The first time they treat a cow, some get an infection—which can sometimes turn very serious—that was simply not seen years ago. I'm convinced it's from our students' lack of exposure to these animals growing up and the missed

In some experts' opinion, the application of antibacterial cleansers in homes has led to children's immune systems' not being properly developed. (© Angela Hampton Picture Library/Alamy)

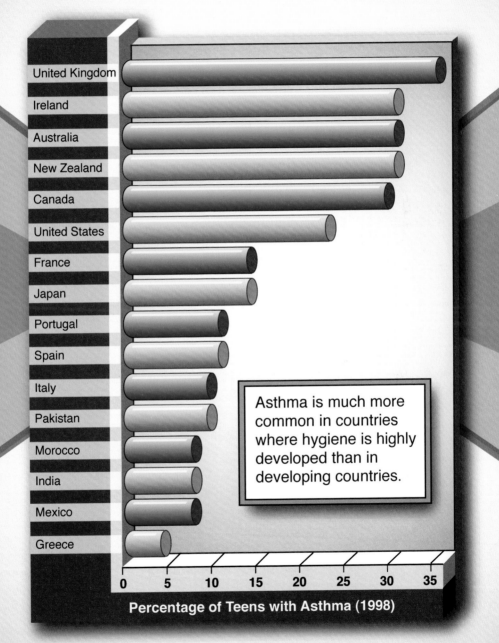

Percentage of Teenagers with Asthma

United Kingdom

Ireland

Australia

New Zealand

Canada

United States

France

Japan

Portugal

Spain

Italy

Pakistan

Morocco

India

Mexico

Greece

0   5   10   15   20   25   30   35

Percentage of Teens with Asthma (1998)

Asthma is much more common in countries where hygiene is highly developed than in developing countries.

Taken from: Jonathan Brostoff and Michael Radcliffe, "The Allergy Epidemic," November 27, 2006. www.allergyclinic.co.uk/epidemic.htm.

opportunity to build up immunity to the bacteria that are natural to their environment."

There is mounting scientific evidence to support Bowman's personal experience. Studies performed in The Netherlands, New Zealand, Austria, and, more recently, the United States have shown that children who grow up on farms or in rural areas have a lower risk for developing allergies and asthma than children in "cleaner" environments.

Farmers' Kids Are Safer

The medical journal *Lancet*, for example, reported in 2001 on a European investigation that found that children exposed to a farm environment in the first year of life had significantly lower rates of asthma, atopy, and hay fever than did those exposed later in life. Other studies have suggested that it is not farm life per se, but our Western lifestyle that is somehow depriving children's developing immune systems of sufficient exposure to infectious agents that might nurture "allergy protective" infection-fighting immune responses.

In one well-known study, researchers compared the prevalence of allergies in the East German and West German populations before and after the two countries' reunification. Before the reunification, East Germany was relatively unpolluted. It had more children growing up on farms and in larger families—and much lower rates of allergies than were found in West Germany. After reunification, however, East Germany developed a more western culture and its rate of allergies rose to resemble those of West Germany.

"Mother Nature is good to us," noted Eliot Epstein, chief environmental scientist at Tetra Tech (Framingham, Mass.), and an adjunct professor at the Boston University School of Public Health. "She protects us by having indigenous organisms that can survive and proliferate and that can overcome the pathogens that cause us harm.

If you get rid of these organisms, you take away some of our protection. That is not to say that dirt is good, but too much cleanliness is probably not necessary either," Epstein added.

Some Doubts

Not everyone in the scientific community, however, buys into the "hygiene hypothesis." "The idea that we can be 'too clean' and that we're creating these mutant 'super-bugs' through the overuse of disinfectants simply has no basis in reality," said Chuck Gerba, professor of environmental microbiology at the University of Arizona. "Some people compare it to the antibiotic resistance that is caused by an overuse of antibiotics, which is a real problem. But it's just not an analogous situation."

"If it were true that bugs could develop resistance to chlorine and other disinfectants, then waste treatment plants would be put out of business. The average waste-water treatment plant uses more chlorine in a day than a single consumer could use in 10,000 years," he said.

People also make the mistake of thinking we have increased the amount of disinfectants we use in this country, Gerba said. "But we don't have more disinfectants," he said. "We've just made them more convenient to use." The history of Western culture, Gerba believes, supports his contention that "you just can't be too clean."

"Conventional wisdom assumes that we are healthier today because of innovations in medicine, such as vaccines and antibiotics," he said. "And there's no question that they have improved our lives." But their contribution, Gerba said, is dwarfed by the advances made in personal hygiene practices and cleanliness over the past 200 years. "In the early 1800s, life in America took place in extraordinarily filthy conditions—not unlike what you'd find in many developing countries today," he said.

Some people went their whole lives without ever taking a bath. Meanwhile, open sewers and waste piled up in streets, which led to legendary stench, particularly in warm weather. These conditions only improved thanks to the "sanitary movement" and the creation of Public Health authorities to regulate wastewater collection and water supply.

"If you go back 100 years, we were still in the age of epidemics," Gerba said. "They were largely ended by filtration and by treating drinking water. So, in that sense, chlorine has probably saved more lives than any other substance in human history."

"Access to clean water and sewers lowers death rates," Gerba added. "In fact, research has found that there is a direct correlation between soap and water consumption and childhood mortality. So to say we're too clean—why, that notion would have Louis Pasteur turning over in his grave," Gerba said.

Even if they see some truth in the "hygiene hypothesis," many scientists acknowledge that the increase in soap and water alone probably doesn't account for the dramatic increase in allergies and asthma. They say that everything from hurricanes to increased public awareness could play an equal or greater role in the growth in allergic diseases, and that the hygiene hypothesis will remain largely that—a hypothesis—until a more research is conducted.

Undercleaning Homes Causes More Allergies

National Institute of Allergy and Infectious Diseases

The National Institute of Allergy and Infectious Diseases (NIAID) warns that mold grows easily in places where there is moisture or dampness, especially in places like showers, basements, and closets. The organization also says that dust mites are especially found in homes and offices, and that house pets are one of the most common sources of allergic reactions. In the following excerpt, NIAID suggests, as a preventive measure, cleaning and paying special attention to corners of the house where allergens could easily lurk. The National Institute of Allergy and Infectious Diseases is a division of the U.S. Department of Health and Human Services, dedicated to research on and better understanding of allergic diseases.

An allergy is a specific reaction of the body's immune system to a normally harmless substance, one that does not bother most people. People

SOURCE: National Institute of Allergy and Infectious Diseases, "Airborne Allergens: Something in the Air," NIH Publication No. 03-7045, April 2003. www3.niaid.nih.gov/topics/allergicDiseases/ PDF/airborne_allergens.pdf.

who have allergies often are sensitive to more than one substance. Types of allergens that cause allergic reactions include

- Pollens
- House dust mites
- Mold spores
- Food
- Latex rubber
- Insect venom
- Medicines

Scientists think that some people inherit a tendency to be allergic from one or both parents. This means they are more likely to have allergies. They probably, however, do not inherit a tendency to be allergic to any specific allergen. Children are more likely to develop allergies if one or both parents have allergies. In addition, exposure to allergens at times when the body's defenses are lowered or weakened, such as after a viral infection or during pregnancy, seems to contribute to developing allergies.

Mold Allergy

There are thousands of types of molds and yeasts in the fungus family. Yeasts are single cells that divide to form clusters. Molds are made of many cells that grow as branching threads called hyphae. Although both can probably cause allergic reactions, only a small number of molds are widely recognized offenders.

The seeds or reproductive pieces of fungi are called spores. Spores differ in size, shape, and color among types of mold. Each spore that germinates can give rise to new mold growth, which in turn can produce millions of spores.

When inhaled, tiny fungal spores, or sometimes pieces of fungi, may cause allergic rhinitis. Because they are so small, mold spores also can reach the lungs.

Mold Growth in the Home

Molds can be found wherever there is moisture, oxygen, and a source of the few other chemicals they need. In the fall, they grow on rotting logs and fallen leaves, especially in moist, shady areas. In gardens they can be found in compost piles and on certain grasses and weeds. Some molds attach to grains such as wheat, oats, barley, and corn, which makes farms, grain bins, and silos likely places to find mold.

Hot spots of mold growth in the home include damp basements and closets, bathrooms (especially shower stalls), places where fresh food is stored, refrigerator drip

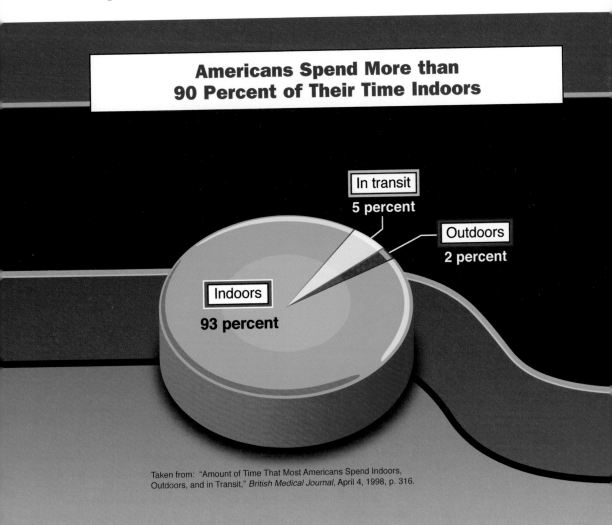

Americans Spend More than 90 Percent of Their Time Indoors

In transit
5 percent

Outdoors
2 percent

Indoors
93 percent

Taken from: "Amount of Time That Most Americans Spend Indoors, Outdoors, and in Transit," *British Medical Journal*, April 4, 1998, p. 316.

trays, house plants, air conditioners, humidifiers, garbage pails, mattresses, upholstered furniture, and old foam rubber pillows.

Molds also like bakeries, breweries, barns, dairies, and greenhouses. Loggers, mill workers, carpenters, furniture repairers, and upholsterers often work in moldy environments.

Like pollens, mold spores are important airborne allergens only if they are abundant, easily carried by air currents, and allergenic in their chemical makeup. Found almost everywhere, mold spores in some areas are so numerous they often outnumber the pollens in the air. Fortunately, however, only a few dozen different types are significant allergens.

In general, *Alternaria* and *Cladosporium* (Hormodendrum) are the molds most commonly found both indoors and outdoors in the United States. *Aspergillus, Penicillium, Helminthosporium, Epicoccum, Fusarium, Mucor, Rhizopus,* and *Aureobasidium* (*Pullularia*) are common as well.

There is no relationship, however, between a respiratory allergy to the mold *Penicillium* and an allergy to the drug penicillin, which is made from mold.

Dust Mite Allergy

Dust mite allergy is an allergy to a microscopic organism that lives in the dust found in all dwellings and workplaces. House dust, as well as some house furnishings, contains microscopic mites. Dust mites are perhaps the most common cause of perennial allergic rhinitis. House dust mite allergy usually produces symptoms similar to pollen allergy and also can produce symptoms of asthma.

House dust mites, which live in bedding, upholstered furniture, and carpets, thrive in summer and die in winter. In a warm, humid house, however, they continue to thrive even in the coldest months. The particles seen floating in a shaft of sunlight include dead dust mites and

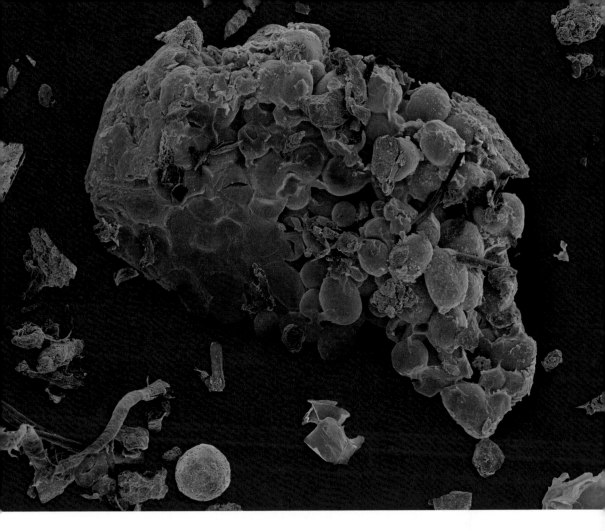

their waste products. These waste products, which are proteins, actually provoke the allergic reaction.

House Dust

Rather than a single substance, so-called house dust is a varied mixture of potentially allergenic materials. It may contain fibers from different types of fabrics and materials such as

- Cotton lint, feathers, and other stuffing materials

- Dander from cats, dogs, and other animals

- Bacteria

- Mold and fungus spores (especially in damp areas)

A microscopic view of dust mite fecal pellets. Dust mites are responsible for 80 to 90 percent of allergenic compounds found in everyday household dust. (© Visuals Unlimited/Corbis)

- Food particles

- Bits of plants and insects

- Other allergens peculiar to an individual house or building

Cockroaches are commonly found in crowded cities and in the southern United States. Certain proteins in cockroach feces and saliva also can be found in house dust. These proteins can cause allergic reactions or trigger asthma symptoms in some people, especially children. Cockroach allergens likely play a significant role in causing asthma in many inner-city populations.

Animal Allergy

Household pets are the most common source of allergic reactions to animals.

Many people think that pet allergy is provoked by the fur of cats and dogs. Researchers have found, however, that the major allergens are proteins in the saliva. These proteins stick to the fur when the animal licks itself.

Urine is also a source of allergy-causing proteins, as is the skin. When the substance carrying the proteins dries, the proteins can then float into the air. Cats may be more likely than dogs to cause allergic reactions because they lick themselves more, may be held more, and spend more time in the house, close to humans.

Some rodents, such as guinea pigs and gerbils, have become increasingly popular as household pets. They, too, can cause allergic reactions in some people, as can mice and rats. Urine is the major source of allergens from these animals.

Allergies to animals can take 2 years or more to develop and may not decrease until 6 months or more after ending contact with the animal. Carpet and furniture are a reservoir for pet allergens, and the allergens can remain in them for 4 to 6 weeks. In addition, these allergens can stay in household air for months after the animal has been removed. Therefore, it is wise for people with an animal allergy to check with the landlord or previous owner to find out if furry pets lived on the premises.

Chemical Sensitivity

Some people report that they react to chemicals in their environments and that these allergy-like reactions seem to result from exposure to a wide variety of synthetic and natural substances. Such substances can include those found in

- Paints
- Carpeting
- Plastics
- Perfumes
- Cigarette smoke
- Plants

Although the symptoms may resemble those of allergies, sensitivity to chemicals does not represent a true allergic reaction involving IgE [immunoglobulin E] and the release of histamine or other chemicals. Rather than a reaction to an allergen, it is a reaction to a chemical irritant, which may affect people with allergies more than others.

> **FAST FACT**
>
> Experts who support the hygiene hypothesis recommend going light with spring cleaning. Instead of using pure bleach to clean surfaces, for example, they recommend diluting the bleach to a 10 percent solution.

Preventing In-Home Allergies by Cleaning

If you have dust mite allergy, pay careful attention to dust-proofing your bedroom. The worst things to have in the bedroom are

- Wall-to-wall carpet
- Blinds
- Down-filled blankets
- Feather pillows
- Stuffed animals

- Heating vents with forced hot air
- Dogs and cats
- Closets full of clothing

Carpets trap dust and make dust control impossible.

- Shag carpets are the worst type of carpet for people who are sensitive to dust mites.
- Vacuuming doesn't get rid of dust mite proteins in furniture and carpeting, but redistributes them back into the room, unless the vacuum has a special HEPA (high-efficiency particulate air) filter.
- Rugs on concrete floors encourage dust mite growth.

If possible, replace wall-to-wall carpets with washable throw rugs over hardwood, tile, or linoleum floors, and wash the rugs frequently.

Reducing the amount of dust mites in your home may mean new cleaning techniques as well as some changes in furnishings to eliminate dust collectors. Water is often the secret to effective dust removal.

- Clean washable items, including throw rugs, often, using water hotter than 130 degrees Fahrenheit. Lower temperatures will not kill dust mites.
- Clean washable items at a commercial establishment that uses high water temperature, if you cannot or do not want to set water temperature in your home at 130 degrees. (There is a danger of getting scalded if the water is more than 120 degrees.)
- Dust frequently with a damp cloth or oiled mop.

If cockroaches are a problem in your home, the U.S. Environmental Protection Agency suggests some ways to get rid of them.

- Do not leave food or garbage out.
- Store food in airtight containers.
- Clean all food crumbs or spilled liquids right away.

Try using poison baits, boric acid (for cockroaches), or traps first, before using pesticide sprays.

If you or your child is allergic to furry pets, especially cats, the best way to avoid allergic reactions is to find them another home. If you are like most people who are attached to their pets, that is usually not a desirable option. There are ways, however, to help lower the levels of animal allergens in the air, which may reduce allergic reactions.

- Bathe your cat weekly and brush it more frequently (ideally, a non-allergic person should do this).

- Keep cats out of your bedroom.

- Remove carpets and soft furnishings, which collect animal allergens.

- Use a vacuum cleaner and room air cleaners with HEPA filters.

- Wear a face mask while house and cat cleaning.

When possible, use air conditioners inside your home or car to help prevent pollen and mold allergens from entering. Various types of air-filtering devices made with fiberglass or electrically charged plates may help reduce allergens produced in the home. You can add these to your present heating and cooling system. In addition, portable devices that can be used in individual rooms are especially helpful in reducing animal allergens.

An allergist can suggest which kind of filter is best for your home. Before buying a filtering device, rent one and use it in a closed room (the bedroom, for instance) for a month or two to see whether your allergy symptoms diminish. The airflow should be sufficient to exchange the air in the room five or six times per hour. Therefore, the size and efficiency of the filtering device should be determined in part by the size of the room.

You should be wary of exaggerated claims for appliances that cannot really clean the air. Very small air cleaners cannot remove dust and pollen. No air purifier can prevent viral or bacterial diseases such as the flu, pneumonia, or tuberculosis.

Before buying an electrostatic precipitator, you should compare the machine's ozone output with Federal standards. Ozone can irritate the noses and airways of people with allergies, especially those with asthma, and can increase their allergy symptoms. Other kinds of air filters, such as HEPA filters, do not release ozone into the air. HEPA filters, however, require adequate air flow to force air through them.

CHAPTER 3

Personal Experiences with Allergies

Naturopathy Helped Identify Food Allergies

Laura Dontigny Zimmerman

Allergies most often develop during childhood, but they can crop up anytime. In the following selection Laura Dontigny Zimmerman of Seattle, Washington, tells of her experience with the sudden onset of a food allergy. It began with a swelling on her scalp and soon her hair was falling out. Unsatisfied by her treatment at the hands of a medical doctor, she took the suggestion of a friend and consulted a naturopath. Naturopathy is a branch of what is known as "alternative medicine." It emphasizes the natural healing power of the body. Practitioners take the title "Doctor" but are limited in the services they are permitted to offer. Zimmerman says she got an accurate diagnosis of multiple food allergies from a blood test her naturopath performed. By avoiding wheat and other foods she is allergic to, Zimmerman made a full recovery.

Photo on previous page. Allergy sufferers must learn to live with a treatment regimen for their condition. (© Phototake, Inc./Alamy)

I t was February 2005. The first strange symptom appeared. I had my hand in my scalp as I helped my youngest with homework. My fingers fell on this

SOURCE: Laura Dontigny Zimmerman, "My Story," dontigny.com, 2005. Reproduced by permission.

strange lump—soft and pliable. I asked my daughter to look at it. After telling me how completely grossed out she was, she then was able to inform me that it was a whitish lump with redness in the center.

I ignored it for a few days, but it started to spread, and started to ooze, so I went to our family doctor. Ringworm? Eczema? Psoriasis? "I have no idea what that is. I'm sending you to a dermatologist," she said. The very day I was scheduled to see the dermatologist, the inner corner of my eyelids turned red and crusty. The dermatologist said it was some sort of dermatitis, gave me betamethasone valerate to put on my scalp and told me to put Cortaid [hydrocortisone cream] on my eyelids. It started to clear it up a bit and on my recheck, he said that this would now be chronic for the rest of my life. He had no suggestions as to what triggered this and gave me a prescription with lots of refills.

Recurring Problem

The problem was that unless I was putting on the medicine, it never stayed away for very long. And in addition to the red crustiness, my eyelids also swelled on occasion. And to top it off, a solid red, itchy rash appeared on the back of my neck. A friend suggested a naturopath. First thing the naturopath did was to take blood for a food allergy test. The test was not your standard test from an MD [doctor of medicine], who generally will only test for immediate, life-threatening immune responses (IgE). The naturopath tested for both the IgE *and* for IgG, a slower immune response that takes place up to a couple of days of being exposed to the food.

Sure enough, once the tests came back, it showed very high reactions to all dairy, and wheat and moderate reactions to sugar, eggs, sesame as well as a few assorted other things. I cut all of the foods I react to out of my diet and within a couple of weeks, I was almost completely clear. The side benefits to getting rid of all of those things is that my vegetable intake has skyrocketed, I feel fantastic

A naturopath tests an allergy sufferer. Many people say that alternative-medicine techniques help identify allergies. (© Bubbles Photolibrary/ Alamy)

—strong, alert, healthy, and my weight started dropping steadily. In the past, no matter what I did, I was never able to get below a certain weight. Since giving up the foods I react to, I have hit a healthy body weight for me and my weight has stabilized. . . .

Parting from Wheat

The hardest thing for me to give up is wheat. I have always loved to bake—breads, desserts, you name it. But I have discovered some great wheat-free baking books; there are dozens of different types of flours if you just look around. I had never heard of quinoa flour until recently! . . .

Update: October 2005

Well, after creating [my] website, there was a strange, disturbing turn of events. My hair started to fall out! Here I was, with my skin and scalp clearing and now this. My naturopath tried everything—homeopathic remedies, acupuncture—to no avail.

I was concerned especially because she seemed to be running out of ideas. And the time had come for me to take my girls in to have them tested because they say allergies can run in families and they each had some unique symptoms. Jill has always had the "allergic look"— dark circles under her eyes, pale skin, runny nose and chronic sinusitis. Anna has had digestive problems, including gas and diarrhea since she was a baby.

> **FAST FACT**
>
> Dairy and wheat products are among the leading sources of food intolerance.

I stumbled across the website of a food allergy specialist, who happens to practice in my area, so I decided I would go right to the expert and took the girls there. Their blood tests came back almost identical to each other—wheat, dairy, beef and peanuts are their main [allergens].

Gluten Grains as Culprit

But he made a connection that my first naturopath did not. If these blood tests show high in Wheat Gluten (as mine did), that means you should *stay away from all gluten grains*. I had been having barley Pero, oats, Kamut and spelt bread almost daily. The gluten grains are Barley, Rye, Oats, and Wheat (BROW). (Oats do not naturally contain gluten, but all oats manufacturers process oats with gluten-containing grains and they are almost all contaminated.)

So I cut out all gluten and my hair slowly stopped falling out. By the seven week mark (the doctor had said between 6 and 8 weeks), it was completely back to normal.

The Girl Who Is Allergic to Almost Everything

Daily Mail

In the following selection, the *Daily Mail* newspaper tells the story of Laura Weaver, who at the age of thirteen suffers from multiple, highly distressing allergies. Her primary symptom is eczema, an inflammation of the skin that is both painful and disfiguring. Laura's family and school have taken extraordinary measures to try to protect her from the numerous allergens that she reacts to. Laura herself has to spend hours each day applying protective substances to her skin. The *Daily Mail* is Britain's second best-selling newspaper. It was established in 1896.

L aura Weaver suffers a rare skin condition, which has left her allergic to almost everything. The brave teenager has finally been able to go back to school, after staff created a special 'clean room' to protect her from dozens of irritants.

SOURCE: "The 13-Year-Old Girl Who Is Allergic to Almost Everything," *Daily Mail*, dailymail.co.uk, February 29, 2008. Copyright © 2008 Associated Newspapers Ltd. Reproduced by permission.

Laura, 13, is covered in painful, itchy eczema rashes and has to wear bandages 24 hours a day and apply creams every hour. Doctors believe her condition is due to a breakdown of her immune system, which has made her skin hyper-sensitive.

Painful Encounters

Laura's skin flares up after being triggered by any one of a dozen allergies. A whiff of perfume, the smell of an air freshener or just brushing past someone's clothes can leave her doubled over in pain.

She is allergic to all dairy products, some fruit and wheat, all soaps, sprays and perfumes and even reacts to non-cotton clothing and some plastic furniture.

A peanut would send her into lethal anaphylactic shock, and even central heating gives her a high temperature, breathing problems and causes her skin to come up in vivid red rashes.

> **FAST FACT**
>
> Eczema most often appears in early childhood. Nine out of ten people who have eczema get it before they are five years old.

Her parents Lisa, a 41-year-old nurse and Mike, a 49-year-old fire safety consultant, said almost anything can trigger Laura's allergic reactions.

Lisa, of Hereford, said:

> There are very few cases as severe as Laura's. She's allergic to all sorts of foods, to furniture and clothes.
>
> Her skin becomes prickly and itchy, and starts to break and bleed. It's horribly painful and she can have trouble breathing. She also becomes allergic to her own medicines. There are so many allergies that when she gets a reaction, we don't know what has caused it.
>
> It could be someone's clothing who has walked past her in the street which has caused her skin to flare up. You don't know how serious these allergic reactions will be. They can be life-threatening.

Every morning and evening Laura spends two hours pasting on three types of cream.

Daily Prevention Routine

Laura was born with painful eczema covering her whole body, but in the past two years, her skin has become more sensitive than ever.

Every morning and evening she spends two hours pasting on three types of cream, before putting on head-to-toe bandages to protect her skin. But brave Laura is determined to raise awareness of her condition—and achieve her dream of going back to school.

One of the many allergic maladies suffered by Laura Weaver is eczema, an allergic skin disorder characterized by redness, itching, and scaly rashes.
(© Phototake, Inc./Alamy)

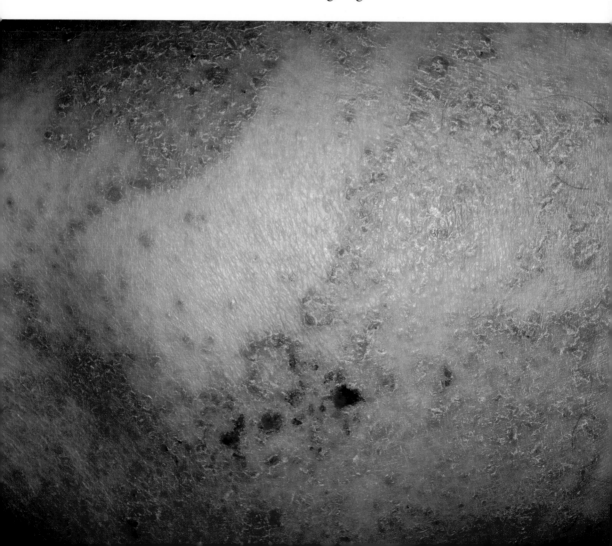

When she tried to go back [in 2007], she lasted just a few hours before her skin became unbearably prickly. She was rushed to hospital and was unable to sleep for a week. She did her school work in a sterilised room at Hereford County Hospital for a year to protect her from the crippling effects of day-to-day germs.

But now her secondary school, Wyebridge Sports College, has created a small "clean room" just for Laura where she can go when she detects irritants in the air.

Laura said [on February 28, 2008]: "I'm loving being back at school and able to socialise, as being in hospital was so isolating. I'm managing two days a week at the moment and it's really good to have the room so I can get away when one of [my] allergies flares up. Even something as simple as the heating or air conditioning can cause a reaction."

Faulty Immune System

Mild eczema affects one in five schoolchildren, making their skin feel dry and itchy. It is thought to be genetic and 70% of children grow out of it by their teens. But severe cases such as Laura's are often accompanied by allergies, which trigger the skin reactions.

Experts believe the reason for this is a malfunction of the immune system—which stops the skin acting as a protective barrier. Harmful chemicals penetrate the skin which, when scratched, becomes infected, causing a temperature and other symptoms such as facial swelling. When Laura has a reaction, she is often taken to hospital for skin treatment, and a strong dose of antihistamines to blitz the infection.

Laura, who raised £1,000 [in 2007] for eczema awareness and has distributed hundreds of leaflets about the condition, has been praised by campaigners.

She added: "It was great to raise the money, because very few people know about severe eczema. I'm already planning to raise more."

Mum Lisa added:

When she was younger children wouldn't play with Laura [because] their parents thought they could catch what she's got. It's very isolating.

It's great she's back at school, but I do worry after her. I tell her to stay away from PE [physical education] lessons. A whole room of people using deodorant would send her over the edge.

This is a debilitating, life-changing condition. But she has had it from birth and is determined to live a normal life, and educate people about it.

There is currently no cure, but her parents are investigating a new type of drug therapy, which suppresses the immune system and has had some positive results.

Laura's father Mike has a very mild case of eczema, and her mum and 19-year-old brother Michael, are unaffected. Margaret Cox, of the National Eczema Society, praised Laura as an "inspiration". She said:

A lot of people are familiar with mild eczema, but Laura is at the very, very severe end of the scale, where you cannot live a normal life.

Her skin does not carry out its barrier function, and instead of keeping out harmful chemicals it lets them in. It is like living with severe sunburn all the time.

All sorts of substances in the air can trigger a painful reaction, which needs to to be treated in hospital, and of course there is a terrible stigma attached to it.

At this level, you have to weigh up the constant risk of infection, with getting on with your life. Laura is so gutsy. She's an inspiration, in her enthusiasm and spirit.

Inconveniencing Others for My Daughter's Safety

Rebecca Fadel King

Parents of a child with food allergies can be put in the awkward position of asking other parents to accommodate the special needs of their child. The following article is written by a mother who recently found out that her daughter has a severe peanut allergy. She expresses empathy for those who may feel put out by having to accommodate her daughter's special needs, but nonetheless feels that her child's safety is paramount.

I've spent a lot of time thinking about what I'll say to the other parents on back-to-school night when my daughter enters first grade. That day is still months away, but I know I need to plan my words very carefully. I need to ask the other parents in the class to protect my daughter's life, and I know there is a good chance that some of them won't feel like participating.

In January [2008] my daughter was diagnosed with peanut and tree-nut allergies. Unlike most children diagnosed

SOURCE: Rebecca Fadel King, "A Plea for My Daughter," *Newsweek*, May 31, 2008. Reproduced by permission.

with severe food allergies, she had never exhibited a visible reaction to the food to which she's allergic. Her allergy was caught by chance, by an allergist who was supposed to be examining her for suspected asthma. Follow-up testing not only confirmed the allergies, but indicated that the peanut allergy is severe.

A Change That Impacts the Entire Family

Over the course of a few days, our family's life changed. Lydia didn't object to not being able to eat nuts—she's never cared for them, and now I know why: they probably made her mouth or throat itch. It's the other adjustments, the ones we didn't expect, that are harder.

The Chinese buffet restaurant where we like to take the kids for dinner? Off-limits, forevermore. Chinese food is often cooked in peanut oil, and the risk of cross-contamination at a buffet is uncontrollable. Ice-cream parlors, bakeries and doughnut shops are also forbidden. But the hardest thing so far has been watching a 5-year-old practice injecting her own thigh with epinephrine, the lifesaving medication she'll have to take, quickly, if she ever eats a trace of peanut by accident.

> **FAST FACT**
>
> Peanut or tree nut allergies affect approximately 0.6 percent and 0.4 percent of Americans, respectively, and cause the most severe food-induced allergic reactions.

Lydia will never be able to go to a birthday party without bringing her own home-made cupcake. Every time she eats in a restaurant, she'll have to bring a card detailing her allergies and pray the chef takes her seriously. I don't want to think about when she's a teenager, too cool to even ask what's in food she's being offered. For now, she can't go over to a friend's house without the friend's mother's being fully versed in Lydia's emergency protocol. It's enough work keeping kids entertained and fed; staving off anaphylactic shock may be more than some moms are willing to sign on for.

But Lydia did all these now forbidden things before she was diagnosed. She ate cookies made on equipment shared with nuts. She went on playdates and ate whatever snack was offered her. She sat across the table from a brother whose hands were sticky with peanut butter. She never had a problem before; what's different now?

What's different is that now we know that there are antibodies lurking in her blood that will overreact if they come in contact with the smallest bit of nut. We're not being insanely cautious now; we were insanely lucky before. Peanut allergies are like mutual funds: past performance is

Parents of children with peanut allergies must pay close attention to their child's diet. (Emily Zoladz/Newhouse News Service/Landov)

no guarantee of future results. Lydia's last reaction to nuts may have been itchy lips. Her next could kill her.

Asking for Help

Or not. She could break out in hives, or throw up. There's simply no way to know. In a way, that complicates matters. Although death by peanut is a real possibility, it is a relatively rare one. And people are reluctant to be inconvenienced to prevent an event they don't really believe will happen anyway. While scouring the Internet to learn about my daughter's condition, I came across a screed by a man furious at being denied peanuts on airline flights because of those whiny allergic people. Some readers commented on his selfishness. But several others cheered him on, suggesting ways he might "get back at" the whiners by surreptitiously exposing them to peanuts.

I've never met someone willing to express such malice to my face. But I have seen parents roll their eyes when another parent stands up at back-to-school night and begins, "My child has a nut allergy. . . ." A few months ago, I myself groaned inwardly when I learned that the one classmate my daughter wanted at her birthday party was the one with a food allergy. I thought it odd that the girl's family ate quietly in a different area of the restaurant where we held the party. Now I know why: they wanted to be nearby with an EpiPen [epinephrine self-injector], just in case. They didn't know me and didn't want to put me in the position of having to ensure their child's safety.

I don't want to ask that of other parents, either, I don't want to ask them to deny their children their favorite treats because my child can't be near peanuts. I don't want them rolling their eyes at me, or, God forbid, at my child. I hate to ask for their help, but I will, because I cannot keep my daughter safe by myself.

My Allergy to Latex Gloves Impacted My Life and Career

Abby Wojahn

Latex is a rubbery material derived from the milky sap of various plants. It is often used to make tight-fitting gloves for use in medical settings. In the following selection, Abby Wojahn tells of how an allergy to latex nearly ended her nursing career. At first, she says, her only symptom was itchy hands. Eventually, however, other symptoms that she could not ignore developed, including asthma. Abby Wojahn is a registered nurse who lives and works in Wisconsin. She frequently writes about medical topics, including latex allergy.

M y battle with latex allergy started in nursing school. I began having contact dermatitis when I wore powdered gloves (both latex and non-latex) but I ignored it since most of the other students had it too. This continued for about 2 years. I finally paid attention when I had crusts a quarter inch deep on the backs of my hands and in between my fingers. My hands

SOURCE: Abby Wojahn, "My Story," *Suite 101*, May 15, 2001. Reproduced by permission.

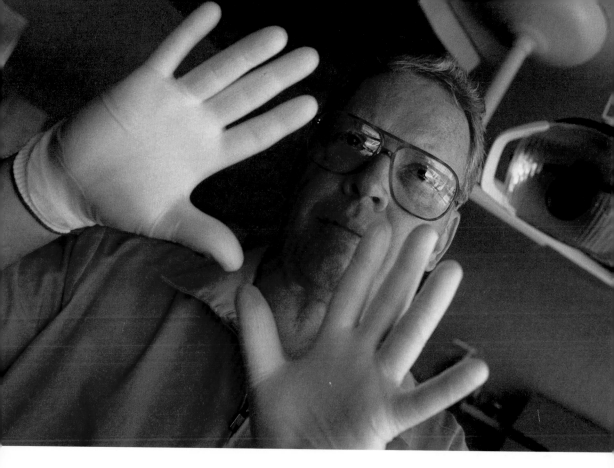

A dentist wears latex gloves over these cloth liners to reduce risk of latex allergies. Latex allergies are reaching epidemic proportions among medical workers. (AP Photo/ John Bazemore)

itched like crazy after wearing gloves and were red and inflamed all the time. When my friends and family started commenting on how bad they looked, I went to see my doctor. The diagnosis was what I expected . . . dermatitis. Nothing was said about an allergic reaction. I got hydrocortisone cream and within a few weeks my hands looked better. I stopped wearing powdered examination gloves but I worked in ICU [intensive care unit] and used sterile gloves every 1–2 hours throughout every shift. The only sterile gloves we had were powdered latex.

The next step was small circular rashes on my arms. This time, I was diagnosed with ringworm and got an antifungal cream, along with more hydrocortisone cream. The rashes went away where I used the cream but I started breaking out on my hips and legs from the elastic in my underwear. I also noticed red, raised, itchy areas in strange places that seemed worse at work and got better when I

PERSPECTIVES ON DISEASES AND DISORDERS

was off for a few days. I had these on my eyelids, my right arm and my left foot. About this time, the employee health nurse sent out a latex allergy survey. I responded "yes" to almost every question that began "Have you ever had a reaction from . . . ?" I talked to my primary doctor, was referred to an allergist and had testing for latex allergy. The blood test for antibodies was negative but the skin prick test was positive. That, combined with my history, convinced my allergist that I had a latex allergy.

I went back to work and started wearing vinyl gloves under the powdered latex gloves when I had to do sterile procedures—which continued to be throughout every shift. I thought I was protecting myself by keeping the latex from touching my skin. I tended to ignore my symptoms, even though I knew better. After all, I was a nurse; I was supposed to take care of my patients first. It turned out that my lack of education and denial would be my undoing.

Onset of Asthma

A few months later, I started noticing that I was wheezing and felt short of breath most of the time. Carrying groceries up the stairs to my apartment was uncomfortable because I couldn't breathe. The defining day came when I tried swimming laps in the pool. I had been a competitive swimmer from age 8–18 and had never had trouble breathing. That day in the pool, I started wheezing after just a few strokes.

Back to the allergist again. I had pulmonary testing and he diagnosed me with asthma. Since I had never had asthma symptoms before, he said it was related to the latex allergy and told me in no uncertain terms that I could not continue working with patients. I had no idea that while I was protecting my skin from the latex gloves, I was still breathing in the powder. My life was turned upside down. I had never had serious health problems, so going home with my big bag of inhalers and equipment was scary in itself . On top of that, my career was over. I had wanted to be a nurse since I was 4 years old. I didn't know who I was without nursing.

No More ICU

My manager was willing to let me try a nurse clinician position in the ICU since I was working on my master's degree. I made it four months. (During that time, I was able to get the unit to switch to synthetic sterile gloves.) One day, I picked up a left-over package of latex gloves to throw it away. I immediately had an asthma attack, felt my lips get tingly, got very lightheaded and had welts around my eyes. My manager marched me down to the employee health nurse and that was the end of my time in the ICU.

> **FAST FACT**
>
> According to a 1997 report by the Centers for Disease Control and Prevention, health-care workers suffer from latex allergies at rates two times greater than the general population.

I now react almost everywhere in the hospital. I'm also more sensitive to latex at home and in public places, so I carry my inhaler and Epi-pen everywhere I go. I'm convinced that my lack of education and my denial directly contributed to the escalation. Please learn from my experience—if you have symptoms that sound similar to mine, stop your latex exposure now. Your life is worth it!

Saving My Own Life

Steff Sanchez

Severe food allergies impose severe constraints on a person's life. In the following selection, student journalist Steff Sanchez discusses how she has coped with multiple attacks of anaphylaxis, a potentially deadly systemic condition that results from severe allergies. As a young adult, she has to prepare each day to save her own life in case she encounters peanuts, peaches, or other possible allergens. She even has to check on what her boyfriend has eaten before she kisses him. Steff Sanchez is a senior at the University of Missouri, where she is working toward a bachelor's in journalism and a bachelor of arts in Latin. Allergy awareness is an important cause for Steff, who wrote the article from which this selection comes while interning in London with the British branch of MSN, the Microsoft media network.

Fork poised to mouth, I dig in and take a bite. Within seconds, I know that it is going to be a very awful day. It starts with a tickle of the back of the

SOURCE: Steff Sanchez, "Living with a Severe Allergy," UK.MSN, http://style.uk.msn.com, May 2008. Copyright © 2008 Microsoft. Republished with permission.

throat, a slight swelling of the tongue. I feel a lump develop as I start to swallow. It's time to put down the fork and pick up the phone: "I need an ambulance".

In rolling the genetic-dice, I was lucky in many respects. However, my parents passed on a possibly fatal trait: I have an anaphylactic allergy to nuts (and oddly enough, to peaches). What does this mean? Anaphylaxis occurs when the body's immune system takes a typically harmless substance (such as food or a bee sting) and attacks it. The skin itches and puffs up; uncomfortable for sure. More seriously, blood pressure drops dangerously low and the airways start to swell shut. Without medical treatment, a sufferer could be dead in minutes. This is a fate that I have been lucky to escape more than once.

Diagnosed when I was about three or four years old, I have dealt with this problem essentially my whole life. My allergies constantly affect my actions through simple things that many people take for granted. Whether it is spending twice as long at the grocer or avoiding a literal kiss of death from my boyfriend, allergies dictate large portions of my life.

Don't Leave Home Without It

Examine the contents of your pockets or purse. What can't you leave home without? Is it your bank card, maybe a set of house keys? Why not try an auto-injecting 0.3 mg shot of adrenaline? Anaphylaxis is no joke and if caught in an emergency my Epi-Pen [epinephrine self-injector] is my best friend. Epinephrine, commonly known as adrenaline, is used to suppress the immune system and combat the reaction to the allergen.

Once a reaction is triggered, I shoot myself in the thigh before rushing to the emergency room for medical care. Time is essential, and in a crisis I need easy access to my shot. Not only do I always keep one on my person, I have one stashed at my boyfriend's flat, my kitchen and my car. When on holiday, I bring two extras in my suit-

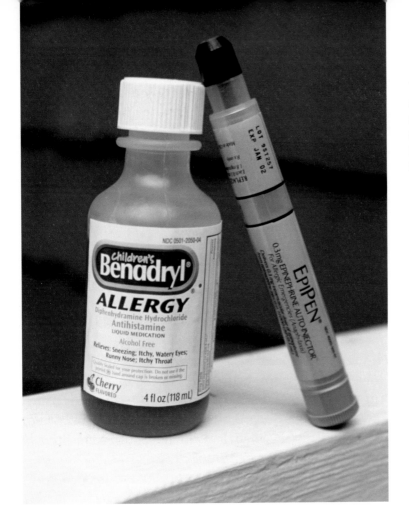

The best friends of an allergy sufferer are allergy medication and the Epi-Pen auto-injector. (© Erik Freeland/Corbis)

case. Believe me, it is better to be over prepared than caught in an emergency without a lifeline.

I am a label reader. A thorough label reader. While caloric intake is important, it is honestly not my most pressing concern. Ingredients are more important as a consumer with allergies. If I miss a beat, I could earn myself a trip to the emergency room. Even when purchasing familiar brands, it is important to re-check the package every time I stop by the market. Products may change their ingredients without warning, (i.e. "Great New Taste!") and it is important to be informed. Luckily, store bought food is packaged with helpful allergy warnings. Not only does it list common triggers such as nuts, wheat and milk, but even food processed on the same machinery will be labelled as "not suitable". Cross contamination can be a problem, so it is important to read every bit of information.

Hard on Romance

One place that my allergy [affects] me hardest is in my love life. Not that I am interested, but random snogs [kisses] are thoroughly off-limits. Believe me, explaining the whole "I could die if you've been snacking on nuts" bit is not only embarrassing, it is surely a buzz kill. Personally, I would rather play it safe with my health than let some lecherous could-be liar have their way. Luckily, I have a long-term boyfriend that understands.

I will never make him choose between me and a tin of almonds. However, he understands that if he does indulge, I won't come within ten feet—and definitely no hugs and kisses unless he's thoroughly washed his hands and brushed his teeth. And rinsed with mouthwash. I am not exaggerating when I say that people have literally died from contaminated smooches.

Eating out also becomes problematic. Food options are limited (as both a vegetarian and a nut-allergy sufferer) and restaurants are not always as responsible as they should be. Even if you put it bluntly, there is no guarantee that I won't be mortally wounded from pine-nut infested marinara sauce. Believe me, it's happened. I actually broke up my older sister's high school graduation celebration with a trip to the hospital after a negligent waiter "promised" that he asked the chef about nut content.

It was only a few months ago, midway through my twentieth year on this earth, that I ate my first peanut butter and jelly sandwich. No, I did not discover a miracle drug that spared my lungs from shutting down. The solution was something entirely simpler: sunflower-seed based spread. Virtually identical in texture (including whole kernels for the "chunky" variety) and taste, this is a product that literally brought tears to my eyes. As a little girl, I was forced to watch the other kids enjoying their sandwiches, feeling slighted by my genetic fate. No more.

As allergy awareness increases, substitutes for the fatal foods are now flooding the market. Soy and sunflower-based products are excellent alternatives to everything from peanut products (such as oil and peanut butter) to milk.

Speaking Out

In the end, it is my own responsibility to be my own allergy advocate. Since I was very young, I have been responsible for being aware of my environment. I double-check what I am about to eat, leaving it alone if there is any doubt. I let those that I am living with know immediately that they have to be careful. Leaving walnut remains on the counter after cooking is simply not an option. If I fail to speak up, there could be deadly consequences. Moreover, I teach everyone that will be spending a lot of time with me, be it flatmate or friend, how to use an epinephrine shot. If an allergy leaves me unexpectedly unconscious, I need them to know the best way to help save my life.

> **FAST FACT**
>
> Food Allergy Awareness Week takes place in May and is a weeklong effort to raise awareness about food allergies.

As more people become aware of anaphylaxis, I find my life getting gradually easier. It is not only simpler to identify products that use nuts, but also to find dietary alternatives to fill in the gap. Acquaintances are less frequently insulted when I refuse homemade baked goods, understanding what I mean when I say "anaphylaxis". I've figured out how to keep myself safe, and learned to accept my allergy. Even though I am an allergy sufferer doesn't mean I have to suffer.

GLOSSARY

allergen   A normally harmless substance that triggers an allergic reaction.

allergic rhinitis   A formal term for so-called hay fever. (*See also* seasonal allergic rhinitis)

allergy   A hypersensitive reaction of the immune system to one or more specific substances that, in most people, cause no distress.

anaphylaxis   A life-threatening allergic response that may include a rapid drop in blood pressure, racing heartbeat, and a swelling of the throat or airways.

antibodies   Special Y-shaped proteins produced by immune system cells that circulate in the blood until they attach to foreign proteins, microorganisms, or toxins in order to neutralize them.

antihistamine   A type of medication that prevents symptoms of congestion, sneezing, and itchy, runny nose by blocking histamine receptors. (*See also* histamine)

asthma   A narrowing of the airways, often brought on by allergies.

celiac disease   A malabsorption disorder characterized by a permanent inability to digest gluten, a protein found in wheat.

dander   Tiny particles of skin that are sloughed off the body and float away or accumulate as dust. Animal dander is a common allergen.

dermatitis   An inflammation of the skin due to direct contact with an irritating substance or to an allergic reaction. Symptoms include redness, itching, and sometimes blistering.

histamine	A chemical present in certain cells throughout the body that is released during an allergic reaction, causing itching and inflammation.
immunotherapy	Treatment of allergic reactions by inducing, enhancing, or suppressing an immune response. This is often done with allergy shots, which allows a control of the amount of exposure to the allergen.
inflammation	Redness, swelling, heat, and pain in a tissue due to, among other things, an allergic reaction.
lactose intolerance	An inability to digest milk sugar, which causes symptoms such as gas, bloating, and abdominal pain, commonly referred to as a milk allergy.
latex	A milky fluid derived from the rubber tree that can be used to make rubber gloves and other products. Some people are allergic to latex.
leukotrienes	Any of several lipid compounds that mediate the inflammatory response. They have been found to play a major role in asthma and other allergic bronchial reactions.
mast cell	A type of cell that releases basophilic granules and substances such as heparin and histamine in response to injury or the presence of an allergen.
seasonal allergic rhinitis (hayfever)	A seasonal allergy to airborne pollen or other particles characterized by itchy eyes, runny nose, nasal congestion, sneezing, itchy throat, and excess mucus.
sinusitis	Inflammation of the sinuses usually caused by bacterial infection or allergy.
skin-prick test	A test to determine if a patient is allergic by placing a drop of the substance being tested on the patient's forearm or back and pricking the skin with a needle to see if a reaction follows.
urticaria	The formal name for hives, itchy, swollen bumps or patches on the skin that appear suddenly as a result of an allergic reaction.

CHRONOLOGY

B.C.   **ca. 3500**   King Menses of Egypt is killed by the sting of a wasp in the earliest known report of an allergic fatality.

ca. 370   Hippocrates, the founder of Greek medicine, observes that some people have a bad reaction to cow's milk.

ca. 300   Practitioners of yoga, the spiritual and physical discipline, develop specific practices in India that include nasal irrigation, possibly as a treatment for allergies.

A.D.   **ca. 170**   Greek physician Galen mentions asthma, a breathing malady often triggered by allergies, in his writings.

1819   Hay fever, or seasonal allergic rhinitis, the most common form of allergy, is first accurately described as a disease affecting the upper respiratory tract by physiologist John Bostock.

1869   Charles Blakely introduces the concept that pollen sensitivity causes hay fever by performing on himself the first positive skin allergy test.

1894   Use of latex gloves in surgery begins.

1902   While performing immunization research, Charles Richet and Paul Portier discover and name anaphylaxis.

1906   The term "allergy" is invented by Austrian physician Clemens von Pirquet.

1912 Immunotherapy, via allergy shots, is established as a way of reducing or eliminating allergy symptoms.

1937 Daniel Bovet synthesizes the first antihistamine drug.

1943 Researcher John Tinterta discovers the connection between the endocrine system, hormone production, and allergies.

1947 Latex gloves covered in cornstarch powder are introduced. The powder is later blamed for spreading allergenic latex proteins through the air in hospitals.

1948 After the discovery of their uses by Philip Hench and Edward Kendall, corticosteroids are first used in clinical medicine as a treatment for asthma and allergic reactions.

1953 Through testing of Judy, a cocker spaniel with a large mast cell tumor, researchers James F. Riley and Geoffrey B. West discover that the mast cell granule is the major source of histamine in the body.

1967 Kimishige Ishizaka and Teruko Ishizaka discover the role of IgE class antibodies as the principal mediator in the allergic reaction.

1982 Professor Bengt Samuelsson receives the Nobel Prize in Medicine/Physiology for identifying leukotrienes, inflammatory molecules released by mast cells, as a major cause of bronchial constriction.

2002 Claritin, a leading prescription allergy medicine, becomes available over the counter; its price drops substantially.

ORGANIZATIONS TO CONTACT

Allergy and Asthma Network/Mothers of Asthmatics, Inc. (AAN/MA)
2751 Prosperity Ave.
Ste. 150
Fairfax, VA 22031
(800) 878-4403
www.aanma.org

AAN/MA is a nonprofit membership organization founded in 1985 to help families in their quest to overcome and maintain control of asthma, allergies, and related conditions. Its Web site includes information for patients, including referrals to physicians, and useful publications and products. Basic information about allergies can also be found on the site.

American Academy of Allergy, Asthma, and Immunology (AAAAI)
555 E. Wells St.
Ste. 1100
Milwaukee, WI
53202-3823
(414) 272-6071
www.aaaai.org

AAAAI is the largest professional medical specialty organization in the United States, representing allergists, asthma specialists, clinical immunologists, allied health professionals, and others with a special interest in the research and treatment of allergic disease. Established in 1943, the AAAAI has more than six thousand members in the United States, Canada, and sixty other countries. The mission of the AAAAI is the advancement of the knowledge and practice of allergy, asthma, and immunology for optimal patient care. The AAAAI is focused on the core values of research, education, and patient care. The organization publishes the *Journal of Allergy and Clinical Immunology*, and its Web site includes links to media related to allergies, as well as other general information.

American College of Asthma, Allergy, and Immunology (ACAAI)
85 W. Algonquin Rd.
Ste. 550
Arlington Heights, IL
60005
www.acaai.org

ACAAI is an organization of allergists-immunologists and related health-care professionals dedicated to quality patient care through research, advocacy, and professional and public education. Their public site, called Allergy, Asthma & Immunology Online, is an information and news service for patients, parents of patients, the media, and employers or other purchasers of group health-care programs.

Asthma and Allergy Foundation of America (AAFA)
1233 Twentieth St.
NW, Ste. 402
Washington, DC
20036
(800) 727-8462
www.aafa.org

AAFA is dedicated to improving the quality of life for people with asthma and allergies through education, advocacy, and research. Founded in 1953, AAFA serves the 50 million Americans with asthma and allergic diseases. Headquartered in Washington, D.C., AAFA has a full-time professional staff and a national network of chapters and educational support groups to provide community-based programs and raise funds for asthma care and research. Information on the Web site is categorized by allergy type.

Food Allergy & Anaphylaxis Network
11781 Lee Jackson Hwy.
Ste. 160
Fairfax, VA 22033
(800) 929-4040
www.foodallergy.org

The Food Allergy & Anaphylaxis Network (U.S. based) is a non-profit organization founded in 1991 and dedicated to food allergy and anaphylaxis. Its mission is to increase public awareness about food allergies and anaphylaxis, to provide education, and to advance research on behalf of all those affected by food allergies. Resources available on the Web site include brochures, information sheets, and guidelines.

Joint Council of Allergy, Asthma, and Immunology (JCAAI)
50 N. Brockway St.
Ste. 3-3
Palatine, IL 60067
(847) 934-1918
www.jcaai.org

The JCAAI was established in May, 1975, as the socioeconomic/political advocate of the American Academy of Allergy, Asthma, and Immunology and the American College of Allergy, Asthma, and Immunology. JCAAI's purpose is to provide a mechanism for keeping allergists/immunologists abreast of the critical socioeconomic issues that impact their practices. The JCAAI represents allergy/immunology in federal and state regulatory and governmental agencies, the Congress, in areas of reimbursement, and in other socioeconomic areas where appropriate. JCAAI serves as a single voice in these areas representing the specialty of allergy/immunology.

La Jolla Institute for Allergy & Immunology (LIAI)
9420 Athena Cir.
La Jolla, CA 92037
(858) 752-6500
www.liai.org

LIAI is a nonprofit medical research institution founded in 1988 and located in La Jolla, California. The institution's main focus is understanding the immune response to infectious agents and cancers and on advancing progress toward the prevention, treatment, and cure of immune system diseases. By unraveling the complexities of the immune system, LIAI researchers are providing critical insights that are moving science closer to the prevention, treatment, and cure of numerous illnesses, including infectious diseases and cancer, as well as immune system disorders such as diabetes, arthritis, and multiple sclerosis. The organization's Web site includes links to related news items, as well as other research material.

**World Allergy
Organization (WAO)**
555 E. Wells St.
Ste. 1100
Milwaukee, WI
53202-3823
(414) 276-1791
www.worldallergy.org

The WAO is an international umbrella organization whose members consist of seventy-seven regional and national allergology and clinical immunology societies from around the world. By collaborating with member societies, WAO provides direct educational outreach programs, symposia, and lectureships to members in ninety-two countries. WAO is expanding its purview in a direct effort to bring together the member allergists and clinical immunologists who are engaged in research and/or practice throughout the world. The organization provides advice and active support to member societies with the mission of building a global alliance of allergy societies that will advance excellence in clinical care, research, education, and training in allergy.

FOR FURTHER READING

Books

N. Franklin Adkinson Jr., John W. Yunginger, William W. Busse, Bruce S. Bochner, Stephen T. Holgate, and F. Estelle R. Simons. *Middleton's Allergy: Principles and Practice.* 6th ed. Philadelphia: Mosby, 2007.

Christina Black, *Mommy, Is This Safe to Eat? A Guide for Preschoolers Allergic to Peanuts and Tree Nuts.* Collierville, TN: R3C Creations, 2006.

Jonathan Corren, Thomas B. Casale, and Daniel C. Adelman, *Manual of Allergy and Immunology: Diagnosis and Therapy.* 4th ed. San Francisco: Lippincott, Williams & Wilkins, 2002.

Milton Gold, *The Complete Kid's Allergy and Asthma Guide: Allergy and Asthma Information for Children of All Ages.* Toronto: Robert Rose, 2003.

Jacqueline Krohn, Frances Taylor, and Erla Mae Larson, *Allergy Relief and Prevention: A Doctor's Complete Guide to Treatment and Self-Care.* Vancouver, BC: Hartley and Marks, 2000.

Frank Kwong, *The Complete Allergy Book: Learn to Become Actively Involved in Your Own Care.* Naperville, IL: Source-Books, 2002.

Donald Y.M. Leung, Hugh Sampson, and Raif Geha, *Pediatric Allergy: Principles and Practice.* Philadelphia: Mosby, 2003.

Dean Metcalfe, Hugh Sampson, and Ronald Simon, *Food Allergy: Adverse Reactions to Foods and Food Additives.* 3rd ed. Malden, MA: Blackwell Science, 2003.

Robert A. Wood and Joe Kraynak, *Food Allergies for Dummies.* Hoboken, NJ: Wiley, 2007.

Merla Zellerbach, *Allergy Sourcebook.* Lincolnwood, IL: Lowell House, 2000.

Periodicals

Angela Cullen, "Breast-feeding Doesn't Ward Off Asthma, Allergies," *Bloomberg News*, September 12, 2007. www.bloomberg.com.

Melissa Kossler Dutton, "Peanut Allergy Backlash," *San Jose (CA) Mercury News*, August 18, 2008. www.mercurynews.com.

HealthDay News, "Traffic Pollution Puts Kids at Higher Allergy Risk," June 19, 2008. www.healthday.com.

Miranda Hitti, "Global Warming May Up Allergies, Asthma," August 5, 2008. www.webmd.com.

Colleen Kaemmerer, "Dairy Allergies and Intolerance," *Suite 101*, 1999. www.healingwell.com.

Mailman School of Public Health, "Childhood with Cats Reduces Rate of Asthma and Allergies." www.medheadlines.com.

Medical News Today, "Stress, Anxiety Can Make Allergy Attacks Even More Miserable, Last Longer," August 15, 2008. www.medicalnewstoday.com.

Nicole Ostrow, "Allergies Alter Kids' Sleep, Play and Concentration, Study Says," *Bloomberg News*, March 16, 2008. www.bloomberg.com.

Pamela Paul, "Allergies at the Dinner Table," *Time*, November 2, 2006. www.time.com.

ScienceDaily, "Eczema and Hay Fever May Be in Decline, but Food Allergies Are Soaring," August 31, 2006. www.sciencedaily.com.

———, "Inflammatory Molecules Released by Pollen Trigger Allergies," February 26, 2005. www.sciencedaily.com.

Laurie Tarkan, "For Adults, Allergies Bring a Surprising Twist," *New York Times*, April 18, 2006. www.nytimes.com.

TaRhonda Thomas, "Parents, Kids, Researchers Team Up to Fight Food Allergies," KUSA-TV, August 18, 2008. www.9news.com.

Washington Post, "Stress, Anxiety Worsen Response to Allergens," August 14, 2008. www.washingtonpost.com.

INDEX